**TURNTABLE LAB DAILY OPERATION**
moving on your weak production.

**TURNT(L)ABLE**

**dj equipment l records l clothing l books**

turntable lab store front
84 e. 10th st. manhattan, new york
212.677.0675

turntable lab online store
http://turntablelab.com

On the Cover: Ramsey Lewis *Maiden Voyage* (Cadet) 1968. Weldon Irvine *Sinbad* (RCA) 1976. David Axelrod *Songs of Innocence* (Capitol) 1968. Idris Muhammad *Power of Soul* (KUDU) 1974. Al Green *I'm Still in Love with You* (Hi) 1972. Ben Sidran *Don't Let Go* (Blue Thumb) 1974. Gil Scott-Heron/Brian Jackson *Winter in America* (Strata-East) 1974. David McCallum *Music: A Bit More of Me* (Capitol) 1967. Les McCann *Talk to the People* (Atlantic) 1972. Jack Bruce *Things We Like* (Polydor) 1968. Eric Dolphy *Out to Lunch* (Blue Note) 1964.

Back cover photo of Idris Muhammad by Duane Michals from the 1974 KUDU release *Power of Soul*.

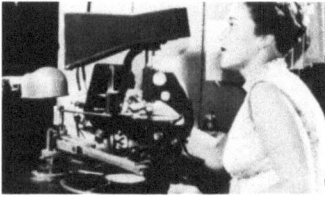

[*step 1*]

[*step 2*]

[*step 3*]

[*step 4*]

[*step 5*]

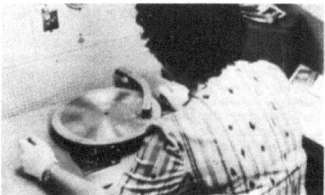

[*step 6*]

| | |
|---|---|
| Editor-in-Chief | Andre Torres |
| Editor | Brian DiGenti |
| Creative Director | Kevin DeBernardi |
| Associate Editors | John Paul Jones |
| | Thomas Rinck |
| Contributing Editor | Andrew Mason |
| Production Designer | Greg DiGenti |
| Production Assistant | Lance Guerriere |
| Accounts Manager | Joy Blameuser |

Contributing Writers — Eothen Alapatt, Joe Allen, Jon Azpiri, John Book, Thomas Sayers Ellis, Alberto Forero, John Paul Jones, Joe Keilch, Andrew Mason, Karl Hagstrom Miller, Mark Randolph, Phill Stroman, Oliver Wang, Jeff Williams, Keith Williams

Contributing Photographers — Eothen Alapatt, Karla Clark, Beth Fladung, Simon Greenberg, Lance Guerriere

Contributing Artists — Ronald "Stozo" Edwards, Alberto Forero

Special thanks to:

The DeBernardi Family, the DiGenti Family, the Torres Family, Angelina, Tom Phillips, Rich Laos, Russell and Gayle (for the inspiration), DJ Citizen Kane, Chairman Mao, Mikael Santos, Edward Applewhite, Rob Corrigan and the Sound Library, A-1 Records, Bobbito Garcia, Scott Harding, Madlib and Stones Throw, Randy Anderson, Thomas Johnson, Kenny Gonzalez, David Mancuso, John Rosado, Mark Smith, Vincent Williams, AJ Woodson, Thad Simerly, David Woodward at DavesRecords.com, Steve Kader, Mr. Supreme, Jason Koransky and *Down Beat*, Stefan Ekstrom, George Mahood and *Big Daddy*, Fred Cohen of the Jazz Record Center, James Gang, Eric Yoon, Steve Ready, Groove Merchant, Anthony at WhereHipHopLives.com, Amir at Fat Beats, Andrew Cope, KC Mack, Thomas Frambach, DJ Phats, Brandon Cady, Dan Berkman at Jump Jump, Chad Burnett, Peter Dolacki, Sean One, John Young, Barney Kulok, Dan Harris, Peter Smithie, Mhat Bernstein, Seth Roehl, and all of the writers and photographers without whom we couldn't have done this. And of course, anyone we missed.

ISBN 978-0-9992127-4-5
© 2001, 2002, 2018 Wax Poetics

Originally published December 2001

Published by Wax Poetics Books
Printed by Lightning Source

# Turning the Tables on Bobbito

by DJ Monk One
photos by Beth Fladung

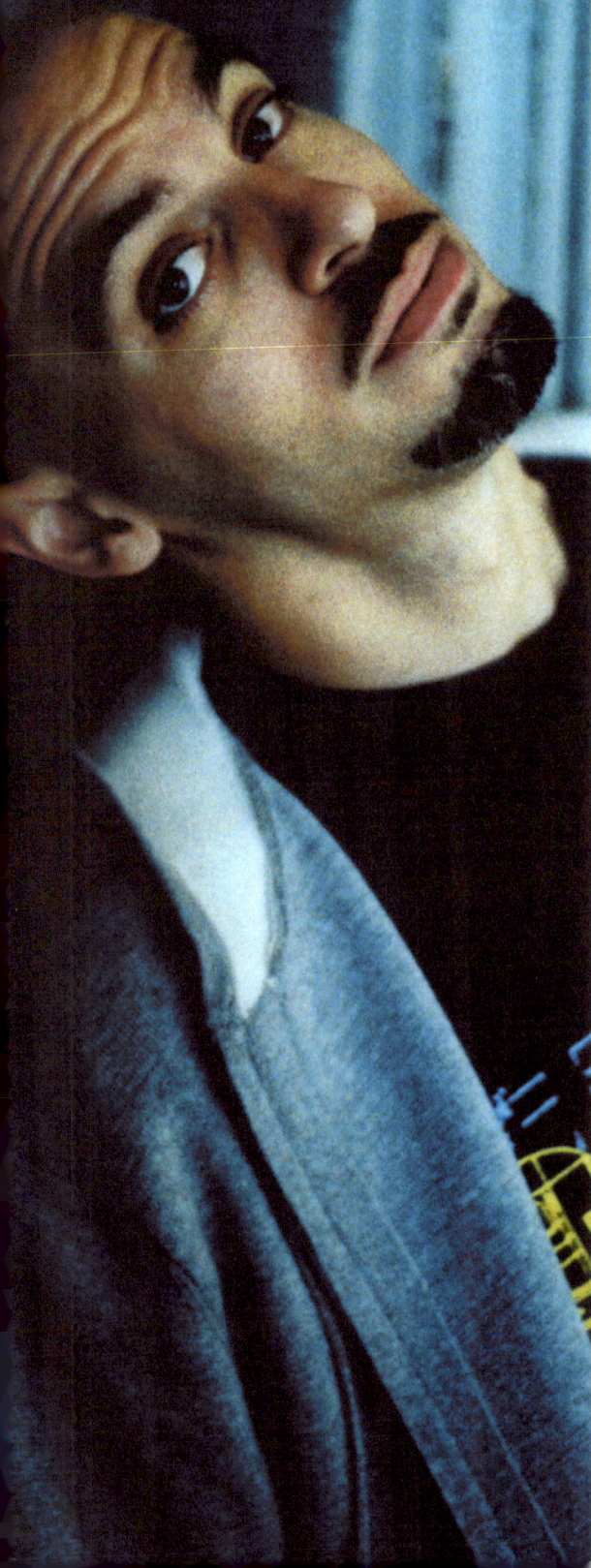

Bobbito Garcia, aka DJ Cucumberslice, is a veritable hip-hop renaissance man. Host of the weekly "C.M. Famalam" radio program on New York City's WKCR, Bobbito is also president of Fruitmeat Records, formerly Fondle 'Em. Since 1995, the producer, poet, and DJ has written the column "Bobbito's Soundcheck" for *Vibe*, spinning joints for the likes of Quincy Jones, Al Green, and Branford Marsalis. WAX POETICS contributing editor DJ Monk One met with Bobbito to turn the tables on him, so to speak.

## Cal Tjader "This Masquerade" (Fantasy) 1977

**BOBBITO:** [*hums along, sings*] "This Masquerade" by George Benson. Well, actually it's a cover. Obviously a vibraphonist; I would guess Cal Tjader—probably not though. I fuckin' love this song. This is totally bringing tears to me. This song reminds me a lot of my dad. My dad played the vibes, first of all, and just recently I got a tape from one of his musician friends of all these jam sessions that he did when I was a kid. It's priceless. I would pay a thousand dollars for it—to hear my dad playing with cats, sounding good, you know? Feeling mad proud.

But in any event he had a pretty diverse ear, which obviously influenced me, and he loved George Benson. He loved George Benson as a vocalist but primarily as a guitar player. I think, similar to Nina Simone, a lot of people don't realize that they were musicians before they became vocalists. Nina Simone was a piano player who was forced one night to sing and then her singing career took off.

It's not Tjader but who is this?

**MONK:** It is Tjader.

**BOBBITO:** Oh cool. My father had this record. That's a hot one there, Monk, that's a real hot one. This record is actually in my mother's house. My dad started letting me take a lot of his Tjader records before he passed, but I never took every single one. I need to see my mom and pick this one up. I did pretty good, I'm one for one!

## Three Dog Night "I Can Hear You Calling" (ABC) 1970

**BOBBITO:** Oh shit. Damn, wait, lemme think who this is. Three Dog Night?

**MONK:** Yeah.

**BOBBITO:** This is fuckin' fat. This is actually on the B-side of "Joy to the World" on the 45. Which is cool 'cause that's the unlimited process of being a DJ. I've had "Joy to the World" in my collection. It's one of the earliest records I have, one of the records I inherited from my sister. I'm continually digging through my own collection. Somebody told me years ago that it's not how many records you have but how well you know your records.

I absolutely love playing in front of my peers and having them come up to me like, "Yo, what is that?" and showing the album cover and having them like, "Damn, I've had that for five or six years!" That's a joy when I research and catalog my own shit and get to know it well enough to do that.

But this is a great tune. Just funky as shit. And to any DJs that want to front on rock music, there's a lot of really funky rock that could easily be played in a set of breaks.

**MONK:** And always has been.

**BOBBITO:** Right, and always has been. But for the "progressive" DJ, well, I've heard certain DJs be like, "I don't play white music." And I'm like, *Well, what the fuck is that*? Music doesn't have a color, you know. If the shit is funky then play the shit and shut the fuck up.

### Tyrone Brunson "The Smurf" (CBS) 1982

**BOBBITO:** This is hot. Just by the snares you know it's an '80s production. Anything before that would've been live drums. How do I categorize this? Kinda like the Black pop synth sound: Cameo, Prince. I felt like they cornered that sound—the bass line, the synth drums. There was Ready for the World, Cherelle…

**MONK:** What's his name? "Haboglabotribin'"—Bernard Wright.

**BOBBITO:** Yeah, Bernard Wright.

I'm blanking on who this is. Are there vocals?

**MONK:** Nah.

**BOBBITO:** I don't have this record. I've danced to it. It's one of those records like "Rain Forest" by Paul Hardcastle. It's totally instrumental, sort of in the same tempo, and every time I play it people come up to me like, "Yo, what is this record?" 'Cause they know it, they've heard it on radio, but there's not a familiar voice to attach to it.

I got to get this. What's the name of that again?

### Trends of Culture "Off & On" (Motown) 1993

**BOBBITO:** This is totally early '90s hip-hop. That drum loop has been used by like 80,000 people. I'm going to guess like Trends of Culture. There was a lot of groups that came out in the early '90s that I felt had really strong instrumentals but there weren't many memorable lyrics or voices that I felt strongly about. But nonetheless, they were relevant groups for the time, part of the whole arena that me and Stretch were presenting to the world on the radio show in the early '90s. Quasi-indie, quasi-unsigned, this whole group of artists that didn't really have a place 'cause they didn't have videos, they didn't have commercial radio-viable songs.

### Idris Muhammad "Loran's Dance" (Kudu) 1974

**BOBBITO:** Put it up a little bit? Somebody sampled that shit. This is a fuckin' beautiful record. I know I don't have it 'cause if I had it I would know it. It's definitely from the golden age of music, probably from '70 to '74… Oh, this is Grover Washington. *Reed Seed*?

**MONK:** It is Grover Washington playing sax…

**BOBBITO:** "Logan's Run"? "Loran's Run"?

**MONK:** Hahaha, yeah, "Loran's Dance," but Idris Muhammad's version.

**BOBBITO:** Is this on the same album as "Crab Apple"?

**MONK:** Nah. One of the early Kudu ones though.

**BOBBITO:** Who used that shit? Tribe used it but they used the other one.

**MONK:** I think the Beasties used that somewhere. But I brought that 'cause it used to be the intro to you and Stretch's show.

**BOBBITO:** What? *This*? No it wasn't.

**MONK:** Yeah it was. The very beginning of this, then there was some static like a radio being tuned and somebody saying *You are now in tune to… blah blah blah*. I remember that shit!

**BOBBITO:** Oh, Stretch used to play [a] record by Sway & Tech that was a medley of different instrumentals, and you would hear the radio dial being turned. One of the samples must've been this. That's funny, man. We used to have so much fun in the early years. The show is still fun now; I don't need to reminisce to think about fun times. But definitely those early years were bugged out 'cause, like, they were such years of discovery.

I think now Sear and I—and I'm sure Stretch on his show on Sundays—we know what we're doing now. We know what we're getting out of it, we know what to expect, we know what the rewards are. But back then there was no way of knowing that Nas, being on our show in February of 1991, would go on to become this multi-platinum artist. There was no way of knowing that.

There was no way to know that we would go to Japan and sign autographs in '95 and find bootleg copies of our show. We were just doing the show at that point not knowing what the ripple effect was or the impact was. And I think that was a good thing because that's what sort of created our carefree attitude on the air and all the kind of bugged out humor. And playing freestyles for two hours without talking, or talking for two hours and not playing music.

We just broke all barriers for what a hip-hop show could be conceived as. I think the reason why is 'cause we just didn't know what the impact was. If we knew that we were eventually going to get on commercial radio or the world was listening we might've been like, *Oh shit, we gotta be serious*. Whereas instead it was like do whatever the fuck we want. Just try to make the best tape so we could listen to it the rest of the week.

### Madlib "6 Variations of 'In the Rain'" (Stones Throw) 2001

**BOBBITO:** Is this the one with Cut Chemist on the other side? I think Madlib straight up is a genius—as Madlib. I'd have to say critically I'm not too crazy about the Yesterday's

It sounds like he got blunted, you know, and just bugged the fuck out, did some shit. Him and Peanut Butter Wolf probably got blunted together, were like, "Yo, let's put this shit out"; PBW was like, "Yeah, let's do it"; Madlib was like, "Okay, let's do it." You know, I'm always down to hear what people are experimenting with in their crib, but I just feel like, I know he could do better. I know he could do better. So I look forward to future YNQ stuff.

## Cenobites "Lex Lugor" (Fondle 'Em) 1995

**BOBBITO:** This is the record that started it all. Not this particular song, but this album was what started Fondle 'Em. This came out in December 1995. Rich King, who was at Big Daddy Distribution at that point, started talking to me in about August of that year, about starting my own label 'cause he heard so many demos that I had.

Recently I licensed a whole compilation of songs to Definitive Jux, a *Farewell Fondle 'Em* comp. There's a Cenobites song off there called "Kick a Dope Verse" that leads [it] off. The Cenobites were fitting to set it off 'cause they were the first group.

I always dreamed of having my own label, but I've always been pretty self-critical and wouldn't have felt confident starting it unless it was going to start with a splash and really make a mark. *The Cenobites* along with *Doomsday* by MF Doom are two of the seminal indie releases on album for the decade, in terms of original sound, interesting lyrics, strong beats, overall concept for an album. So I felt very very proud about this song. This is "Lex Lugor."

I remember when they gave this to me they were like, "This is for nothing else but your show, this is just a promo." And years later it's this crazy indie anthem. There were two pressings of this. The second pressing came out a few years after, had different artwork, a different mastering session. That's an original pressing there, 'cause it has the Fondle 'Em "Christmas" logo. It came out in December—that was kind of like a joke.

The second pressing has the "Kick a Dope Verse" remix, what I call the Battered Whale remix. When I heard the beat I told [Godfather] Don, "This sounds like some abused whales, some abused seals."

Don did all the production on the LP, except for "Mommy." We don't know who did that one. Some kid in Europe, but we had never gotten his name. Keith had given me the cassette to play, and when I pressed it up he couldn't remember who did the beat. I was in Europe one time and this kid came up to me like, "Yo, you used one of my records!" I was like, "What do you want me to do, you know? You got to deal with Kool Keith. I don't know what your arrangement with him is."

With Fondle 'Em, I took the songs from the artist, but if the artist owed money to the producer or the engineer, that was on the artist. That's why I split it 50/50, so I didn't have to deal with anyone but the artist who had given me the record. ◉

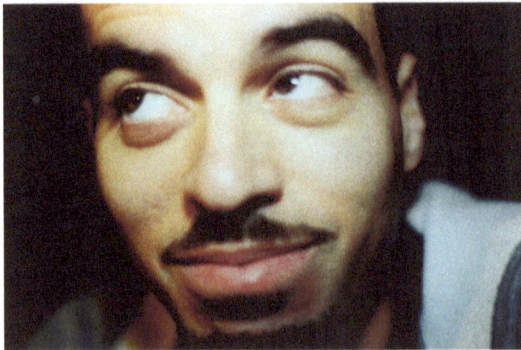

New Quintet productions that he's done. If you compare what he's done as a producer for Medaphoar, Declaime, and for Quasimoto, he has a signature sound that is so interesting and so distinct and so consistent—him and Jay Dee. There's like but a handful of producers that when you see their name on a record you look forward to hearing not the rhymes but the beat, you know? So that's Madlib as a hip-hop producer.

Madlib as this sort of avant-garde jazz producer—I have to say I'm a little more critical of because I expected the same standard from him with regards to YNQ as I did from his hip-hop productions. I have to say I think eventually YNQ will become a tightly knit production sound, but as of right now it just sounds sloppy. It sounds really sloppy. And a lot of people if they don't know jazz music well enough or if they're just catching the Madlib wave and just love anything he does… And I'm not saying this to say I don't think people should buy it or support Stones Throw, but I'm just saying from a critical standpoint YNQ sounds sloppy to me.

# Library of Sound

by Joe Keilch

photos by Simon Greenberg

If you've ever dug for records in New York City, whether it be for old soul and jazz, hip-hop or disco, 45s or soundtracks, you've probably spent some time in the Sound Library. Considered by some to be one of the best record stores in the world. Considered by others to be overpriced and elitist. But, however you look at it, these cats got records. Robert Corrigan, one of the owners of the Sound Library, has mad experience with the world of beats and breaks. Check out his history with buying and selling records and his thoughts on the effects of the Internet and eBay and some of the trends in collecting.

**Tell me about yourself; tell me your name.**

Robert Corrigan, originally from London. I used to come over here buying up records and bringing them back to London. I had a record store in Camden and things kind of went a little crazy over there with my landlord at the place I was renting and everything in my life came to a head at one time. I lost a girlfriend, lost an apartment. I thought, you know, I'm going to come over stateside and stay a bit longer this [time] and, you know, buy up some records and send 'em back. I was doing that for a little while.

[I] met up with Steve [Rob's partner at the Sound Library] and started working with him for a bit, doing record shows, and we ended up buying a lot more than we were selling. It was just soul and jazz.

We never bought any hip-hop then. At the time, hip-hop records were kind of lying around real cheap and there was only one guy there that was trying to sell hip-hop for a little bit of money. But he kind of had it backwards. He only had stuff like Beastie Boys and Public Enemy, which were actually around a lot at the time, and he had other things for way too cheap that should have been a lot more.

[We] started working with Isaac, the owner of A-1 Records, and set up the store with him. [I] was doing all the pricing and that's how the hip-hop section came about in there. [I] started pricing hip-hop records on a global price scale, as to what was going on in Japan, what was going on in Europe.

So we were starting to have records come up on the wall for 20, 30, $40, and nine times out of ten people would walk in there, just local people, and just look at those records on the wall, laughing, saying, "They have no idea what they're doing. They're never going to get this money." And gradually they'd come back in and ask about such and such a record that was on the wall last week and we told them that it'd sold. They'd say, "Who bought it then?" And we'd have to start explaining to people that this is a global thing, it's not just New York people that buy hip-hop, and these records, you just cannot get them anymore. Okay, there's a few lying around in New York. There were so many in New York, there's bound to be a few lying around.

People started to catch on a little bit, gradually, over a couple of years. It took a couple of years for people to start realizing that their collection was worth a hell of a lot more than they thought it was. So we were getting more and more people bringing in stuff they didn't want anymore. Doubles, triples, stuff they didn't care about for whatever reason. A lot of stuff started coming into the store from people walking in knowing we were going to give them a great price for it. So, that's how that place got off the ground and how it got its reputation.

**What time period is this?**

That was five years ago, something like that—don't remember exactly. From there, we were selling our own records in the store as well. Isaac was letting us put our stuff in there on consignment. So if we sold any of our stuff, he'd take a percentage. That's the deal we worked out with him. And a lot of the time, a lot of the records on the wall were eighty to ninety percent ours. Because those kinds of titles weren't coming in as much as we were finding on our road trips.

We were still going on road trips, different states, what have you. Pick up stuff, going to the shows, buying stuff at the shows. We were just gradually building up a nice stock of stuff because we'd been buying ourselves. Getting up at the crack of dawn, going to flea markets and all that started to add up. Anything we did sell, we didn't take any money back, we just put it straight back [into] records.

So we were starting to realize that sooner or later we're going to have to do our own store. Because at that point, instead of working for someone else, if you can do it yourself, do it yourself. We had enough stock to get a little thing started. Get the store open and running.

Basically we parted company with Isaac. We'd employed a couple people while we'd been there so they stayed on. And a couple of the customers that used to come through were offered jobs after we left and they came here. And I hear that [A-1 has] had a fair amount of turnaround since we left.

music we're doing. I don't know about stores in other areas, but as far as soul, jazz, and hip-hop, there really wasn't any store like that.

We get a lot of tourists, dealers from overseas. European dealers bring over a fair amount of European music to trade with us—things that we can get a little more for than they can get over there. It increasingly seems to be the case that stuff is starting to sell for more over there, so it's getting harder to bargain for it. And if we have to put the prices they're charging over there on some of those records, people really would back away from some of those records. Jazz records that are going to be three, four, five hundred dollars. That's a bit steep for the market over here. People are used to everything being cheaper here.

For our store, we took about a month to get it set to open, and it was pretty much an immediate success, as soon as we opened we had people finding us. A lot of people were coming in just amazed at the selection. And, of course, we've been dealing with a lot of producers for a few years. A lot of them were coming to buy stuff we had and gradually things just improved and improved. And we had a very nice looking store, very well presented, organized, clean, tidy. It makes life a lot easier for a customer. I mean, granted you're not going to find a $100 record underneath for $5 because we're a little bit too on the ball for that.

But, at the same time, you can be looking for a particular record and go around to a couple dozen stores and maybe one or two have even heard of it, let alone have it. And you don't have it because you've wasted all this time looking through these stores for a record you just can't get. Now there's a store that you can call us up, ask for something really obscure, and we'll either say, "Yeah, we've got one right now," or "At the moment, we're out of stock but we do get it. Give a call next week." So it's a different type of store from what used to be around, as far as the kind of

**Records are cheaper over here?**

Yeah, it is. I mean we do put things up that, you know, it is a fair price, and actually cheap compared to the European prices. And we're not even talking about Japanese prices. The prices in Japan are all kind of mythical amounts anyway. They change all the time. No one really knows what's going on over there, except people that live there or people that are from there. It's all very vague and there's no websites with their prices on it. There's one, maybe two, websites that price their records on there. These stores with sites don't have prices for what they're selling them for. They keep their cards very close to their chest.

Whereas in Europe, the business has been going on for so many years in soul and jazz and all this stuff; there are tons of people with lists, tons of places you can look for records and compare prices. So we base our business more on what's going on in Europe and what the market will bear in the U.S. than on anything that's going on in Japan. Japan's market is always changing, one month to the next.

They really want the record and they'll buy as many as you've got and then the next month they're like, "They reissued that." And, you're like, "So what?" "Well, nobody wants it anymore." I've never put much into what the Japanese dealers are buying. They could buy ten copies of a record off you and you go out and buy another ten and they come back, they don't want it.

**What percentage of your business is in different genres of music (i.e., what percentage is hip-hop, etc.)?**

In units? Well, the biggest three things are hip-hop, soul, jazz. I think in units, the biggest has to be hip-hop and R&B records because the average price on them is less and we've got a fair amount of new releases and a fair amount of promos and $5 records. It brings down the average. But, in units, that section more than anything else. The biggest section, I guess, money-wise would be soul, followed by jazz. Soul includes funk.

out there. But the other thing about them is the value for money is great. Sometimes 100 to $200 for an album that they only wanted one track on the album. It's not so painful when you're getting a 45. Maybe you like 50% of it. You either like one side or the other. If you like both sides, it's a bonus. There's a value for money thing too.

And because there's still a lot of stuff out there lying around, unlike the albums. The market's draining [albums] out of the country, to Japan and Europe, for fifteen to twenty years. On the 45 front, with hard soul and funk, there's so many copies and so much of it that that will last quite a while longer.

**What can you imagine being the next step after 45s, now that soul and funk albums have kind of been depleted?**

> That's the main feature of our store is you flip through the soul racks or jazz racks and you're not flipping through the same old records you see in every record store in the States. You're flipping over the better ones and obscure ones that you may never have seen before.

After that we do very well with the soundtracks and Latin. The disco does okay although we don't put that much effort into the disco section. That's one thing that A-1 will always be able to beat us on because they have the space for it and have those kinds of collections coming in all the time. And they have the people that know. That area we only scrape the surface, bits and pieces that we always hold.

**What percentage of sales go directly to people for their collections versus people who are going to re-sell?**

The dealer part of it is a tiny fraction. They're no different than a good customer who's serious about their collection. It's not a huge amount of records.

**What's your view on 45s and people's increased interest in them?**

It's definitely come up a lot in the last couple years. There's a lot of kids, from my point of view, next generation kids, that have gotten into the whole record thing, the soul/funk thing, most of them introduced to it through hip-hop, like a lot of us were, and they're gradually digging deeper. They've gone through the albums, they've really done it on the albums. There's not many albums left they haven't heard or can't get a reissue of. So they've started digging into the 45s a little. I mean, I'd like to see how many titles there were compared to albums pressed. There's got to be several hundred 45s for every album made. So, there's an endless supply.

The interest has just jumped. It's the same proportion of good tracks to bad tracks; there's a lot of very bad 45s

Well, the usual way it goes is as these kids get a little bit older they get more into jazz. I reckon they go on to jazz from soul and funk as they get a little bit older. That's usually what happens. Eventually they'll end up on '50s and '60s Blue Note and classical, stuff like that. Soundtracks. But it's a matter of progression. You get sick of stuff after a while. Seems as they never will but sooner or later... They've got their great soul collection. Tons of albums, tons of 45s, but they're sitting watching a movie, like, "I like this soundtrack." So, it's just the way it goes.

**Other than 45s, what are some of the other trends (artists, labels)? What's hot?**

There's certain indie hip-hop records that to us are practically new—only one year, two years, three years old some of them; some of them are five to six years old now, but they seem very new to us—that people are asking for all the time. We don't get asked for DMX, we don't get asked for anything on MTV. It used to be that big artists were popular throughout hip-hop collectors. These days there's a huge divide [in] pop music—hip-hop that's not really hip-hop-y; it's pop. It's not hip-hop music anymore.

It's dividing away from the stuff that's still underground. The stuff that's still sampling. You know, there's some people that think those people are stuck in old days or whatever. There's a lot of indie [records] that people are looking for these days. I'm sure that the more valuable records, from the '90s at least, are all going to be independent. Like from '94 to the end of the '90s are all going to be the independents. Groups that did one or two 12-inches and got a little action from that. The Dilated Peoples. Those kind of people. Already Jurassic. Some of their early stuff is worth a lot of money.

**First record? The Blunt one?**

That's like the third pressing of that.

**Oh, really? I didn't know that.**

Yeah, there's a yellow one under the Unity Committee. Then there's a blue label which was made specifically for a store in London called Mr Bongo. They wanted so many copies, they wanted it so badly, they did a re-press just for them. So, the yellow one, the blue one, then there's the Blunt one, which is different. It's not the same. Track listing, you know. All three of those are valuable though. So, that's a good example.

years through what we've been pricing and what they've learned from coming in the store. Some of these things have ended up on eBay and they've cut out the middleman. *We* used to be the middleman that would give you *x* amount, half cash, two-thirds trade, which is our standard thing. But for certain records that we're selling for $40 and they've seen it go on eBay for 50, 60, 100, they're going to try and get the money on eBay. So we lose out on a certain amount of stock.

But the same people have done that for a little while, dealt with the shipping, bidders that don't come through with the money, dealt with things that made it, "Okay, well maybe it's not worth it as much as I thought it was." And, like, the [extra] amount of time [spent entering records on the computer].

---

**They make a record like Cat Stevens in demand, but they can't make that record valuable. You can't turn around and make a common record valuable.**

---

**What is the effect of eBay on the Sound Library's business and record collectors in general?**

It's got its pluses and minuses. Its biggest plus is all these people I've been talking about who've been coming in our store the last two years and looking at our prices in complete disbelief, thinking we are taking the piss—however you want to put that—we're greedy, we're crazy, all kinds of things they think.

I mean, the fact that we've bought and sold these records for years and got these prices, and they've gradually gone up, they don't see that. But what they see is, they come in and see a record on the wall for $200 and they say how can you justify charging $200 for a record.

eBay comes along and all it takes is two people to want one record—which is not how it works here; we have to sell that record over and over again. All it takes on eBay is two people who want that record now, and they'll go up against each other until you win. Because there's an ego thing, all kinds of things, involved in it, which inflates price, which justifies our prices. Because there's so many records that go for on eBay anything from two to three to ten times what we sell it for.

And that's justified our store a lot. It helps us a lot. People are coming in: "I can't believe how much this went for. I can't believe how much that went for." And we just smile. We're like, "Just watch, next week there'll be five more copies and none of them will go for anywhere near that much." There's very few records which consistently go for a lot like that. It's like every now and again something goes for a ridiculous amount of money.

**What's the downside?**

The downside is that some of the people that bring us records and have learned what records to find over the

The way it really is useful is if it's something that's really in demand, that always goes for a lot of money on there, then I can understand if people put it on there rather than bring it to us.

But the bulk of the records are still coming to us. That period where eBay was taking away certain records is kind of fading off a little bit. Certain people just can't be dealing with it anymore, and they're like, "No, it's just not worth the hassle. I've got fifty records to sell today, another hundred to sell tomorrow. I can't move that many records on eBay." It's just too much hassle. Too many trips to the Post Office. It's just too much. We're getting them back again.

**What about other Internet outlets, like Dusty Groove, or the traditional record stores that have an Internet aspect to their business? Does that help or hurt you?**

I haven't really looked that much. I've looked a little bit here and there and I hear things about Dusty Groove. The majority of the ones I've looked at, the stores have had so few decent titles mixed in with the same old rubbish that every other store's got. I mean, the main thing about our store is that we don't have a big section of Prince, and the 150 Stevie Wonder records. And a lot of stores you have to dig through so much stuff to find—it's not that it's better music—but to find things that are a little bit more obscure. Everyone stocks your Stevie Wonders and Marvin Gayes, and people don't want to have to flick over them every single time they go to a store.

That's the main feature of our store is you flip through the soul racks or jazz racks and you're not flipping through the same old records you see in every record store in the States. You're flipping over the better ones and obscure ones that you may never have seen before.

So, that is the downside of going to a lot of these stores' websites. They put everything on there and you're sitting there reading Al Green, Marvin Gaye, Stevie Wonder. It's not exciting, it's not interesting. Why would I order it off the Internet when I can go down to the flea market, especially the people outside of New York. A lot of those records are easier to find out of New York.

It seems like you sit down in front of the computer, you sit there for three to four hours, and, if you're a customer looking to buy something, you have ordered [only] two or three records. And for the time spent, it ends up not worth it.

We're working on a site ourselves. The way it's going to work is we're going to have just hand-picked titles that are going to go on there. It's not just going to be everything. It's going to be particular records. We want them to be mint, at least mint-minus. We don't want people sending records back; we want them to be satisfied. We want people to be browsing through stuff that they'd be interested in, not just trying to get rid of our cheap stuff. We're working on that, but it's a way off yet. Should be a couple months or so. I don't know.

**You mentioned going out on the road. Is that something you guys still do?**

Oh yeah. A lot of records come through the door, but the premium we have to go on the road. Yeah, we just went to Texas for like four days. I think it's the biggest show in America. Austin, Texas show.

**Do you mostly go to shows or also shop at certain places?**

We try and combine a show, but just hitting the road is good. But, for the average person a road trip is really not worth doing. People talk about going out on the road, "Oh, I found such and such a record for a dollar." But, unless you're buying a lot of records and you're buying them to sell, you do not save the money. It's like with the eBay things, you know. You go out on the road, you've got hotel bills, car rental, or petrol—I mean gas—bills. There's so many expenses and you're eating all this dodgy food and at the end of it you're tired and you feel like shit. And at the end of it, you really only come up with a handful of good records to sell.

If you really sit down and think about it, you might as well go to a couple of stores in New York and just pay the money for the records. I would've come out even, plus I would have had a week at home with my girlfriend or whatever. I could have just watched TV or whatever.

So there's people who've gone out for the Texas show; producers and collectors and what have you. And all the action is in the first couple of hours. You know, if you don't find a couple of good pieces in the first couple of hours, you're going to pay full price for it anyway, or you're just not going to buy anything. [There's been times] where we've bought boxes and boxes of records for the store—we may have got one record for ourselves—and then there's people standing around with a depressed look on their face saying they've looked around the whole place they've bought six records. It cost them a couple hundred in plane tickets, a couple hundred in hotel rooms. It's like, "I can't believe how expensive these records have turned out to be." That's the most common thing.

The whole thing about diggin', the problem is you've got to combine it with something else. You know, if you're visiting family in another state or what have you, mix it in with the local record shops. Spend a little time in there, you might come up with a few things. Going on a buying trip, you have to be able to sell the records that you buy. Just a buying trip, it's not worth it. And plus, the people out there in these stores around the country, they're not as dumb as you would think. That's another thing with eBay. They're looking up everything on the Internet before they price it.

That has actually created quite a problem because ordinary records like James Brown records, which, I'm sorry, are very common. Pretty much all of the James records, they are *common*. They sold thousands and thousands of copies. They're common records. But, you're out in the middle of nowhere but they've got them priced three times what you've got in New York. It's unbelievable. Like down in New Orleans, Meters records down there, they'll pull out a crazy scratched-up copy that you wouldn't get more than $10 for up here because it looks like an ice rink after a hockey game. They've got like $75 on it. And you just want to roll around on the floor laughing. And you know he's probably had it priced like that for three years and you cannot believe these people stay in business. Yeah, eBay's done quite a bit of damage around the country on that front.

**How do particular producers sampling old records affect the value of it? Does Premier using something affect the value?**

When a producer samples a record and it does really well on the radio, then it can make a record we never felt was an

uncommon record into one that we can sell a few copies of. It's not as big a thing as the producers would like to think. They make a record like Cat Stevens in demand, but they can't make that record valuable. It's not going to happen. I don't care. You can't turn around and make a common record valuable. We'll sell more copies of it, but we don't go from selling it from $12 to $50. "Yeah, I want $50 for that." No, it's still $12, but we can sell it easier. We buy a few more copies when we're on the road and they sell. But it's a negligible amount.

And as far as them sampling already collectible records, already rare records, that doesn't change much either. Those records are already expensive and already desirable. It's unfortunate that you get—and we do get it a lot—we got [comments] from producers saying they're making our business, which is kind of crazy. We pick up some obscure little rock record, find a little groove on it, play it for them, they like it, they sample it, they put it out, they make a ton of money off it. We've made nothing off of it. Okay, we bought the record for $10 and sold it for $20. It's meaningless. That's not making money. Where they're maybe charging someone $20,000 for a remix and put the money in the bank.

The best thing about having producers coming in [is] that they want to buy a lot of records. They tend to buy a bunch of things. And it's always cool for customers. Someone comes in here and they're into hip-hop and all that, and they see Premier or someone shopping in the racks, it's a kick for them. Maybe they're asking for their autograph, chat with them for a minute. You know, it's really cool for the customers. And that's always nice.

There's disadvantages to it too. As to, like, handling records. You know, we may have a rare European soundtrack up on the wall at $100 and it's in mint condition. A producer pulls it down, plays it, puts it back, and you look at it later on. It's got fingerprints all over it, some surface knocks. It may even have a gouge in it now. May even have a scratch in it now. It's gone from a $100 record down to nothing. Especially with things like soundtracks, they *have* to be mint. You cannot sell scratched up soundtracks. It's a pretty quiet recording to begin with—orchestral and all that kind of thing. And we've lost plenty of money that way.

Some people when you say anything to them like, "Listen, you're really not supposed to touch the grooves, you know. You're really supposed to handle it by the edges. It's really delicate and all that." And they're like, "Enh."

You know, we've had certain producers who'd buy things and they'll want to trade them back in a week or two later and get some other records. And, they've done the same thing. They've had it for a week and this record is thirty years old. It's mint condition when we sell it and they bring it back two weeks later and it looks 1,000 years old. It looks like it got dug up out of the ground and you just look at them like, "You're shooting yourself in the foot. You know, you're setting fire to money." And they're like, "Enh, it plays alright." There's plenty of downsides to having that element in the store.

## Why do you do this?

It's getting songs for myself that I haven't heard and I wouldn't be able to find if I was working a regular job. I wouldn't get to hear them, I wouldn't find them. Especially with how much I like my reggae. But also, along the other points—hip-hop, soul, jazz—you can't dedicate enough time to it if you've got a full-time job. If you've got a full-time job and a family, then the little you're putting in you'll get out of the music, the records. If you're working with them, a lot of stuff, a lot of tunes become blasé to you. You don't care about them, you've heard them so many times. But that's the little part, that's the downside.

There are certain records that when you are sixteen, seventeen, and you were just starting to discover these things, these tunes, these things were just fantastic to you. There were just great, great stuff. And over the years, it lessens. You know, something you used to hold dear. For example, a lot of people with their jazz started out with Kudu and CTI, you know. If you go back and listen to it, there's a lot of good stuff on those labels. You get blasé about it. You're like "Enh, Kudu. Enh, CTI."

## What about you? Surrounded by music for so long, where do your tastes run these days?

Predominantly reggae. '60s, '70s, early '80s, and some of the new stuff out of Europe. Modern productions like modern dub, modern roots, stuff like that. But really '60s and '70s reggae is my thing these days. And it's such a hard music to collect and it's such a challenge because there's so many tunes, so many 45s, you can't believe what the record says. You have to play every single record to find out what kind of tunes you like.

There's no radio stations really spotlighting the good stuff. You don't really get any help from anywhere. There's no clubs playing it. It's something you really have to devote time and effort to to get anything back out of it.

## Are there certain resources you use, like musicians who were around during that period of time?

Nah, it's basically a part of reggae records; the ones I haven't played before, I play. It's not more complicated than that. If I like it, I like it. The tricky thing is: you find a singer you like, they've done some horrible records as well. You find a producer you like, a label you like, you can't collect on any of those things. You can't say, "Oh, this is this label," because every label's done bad stuff. Unless it's something that they only did three records, then maybe there were three all good records. Generally, you can't go by the label, the artists, anything.

It's really one record at a time thing. ◉

JOE KEILCH (*aka* DJ ELEVEN), *originally from the Bay Area, now reps Brooklyn. He likes talking and writing about music almost as much as he likes getting free records. He's also tickled the keyboard for* Mass Appeal, Platform.net, *and 4080.*

# WFMU Record Fair, New York City  by Andrew Mason

When I was asked if I wanted to share a table at the November WFMU Record Fair I jumped at the chance. After all, this is one of the premier record shows on the East Coast, and here I was given a chance to get in the house before any of the paying customers, including the notorious early-entry hawks. I envisioned the vinyl grabs I would make, candy-from-a-baby style. There was another motivating factor as well; as a radio DJ I'd accumulated piles of ludicrous promotional vinyl, and as a music junky there were numerous failed experiments that were now taking up space in my apartment. What better way to unload all this flotsam than at the fair? And maybe make a buck, too, was a thought not quite in the back of my mind. Of course there were catches: I had to man the table, at least part of the time (i.e., deal with unwashed masses of record geeks), and be there to load and unload. It seemed to be a reasonable trade-off, and I told my contact to count me in.

My leader in this expedition was one Tony Wilds, proprietor of the Wilds Scene website and a guy with a serious wax jones. He gave the marching orders: gather at 11 A.M. outside the site of the fair, a convention center on West 18th Street in Manhattan. Now, the doors weren't even going to open until noon, but I was warned of the jockeying that would take place among the dealers for sidewalk unloading space. I was able to get a reprieve until twelve, at which time I dutifully showed up to find the hall halfway filled with dealers setting up crate upon crate of records on folding tables. Tony had been merciful enough to show up at my crib that morning to pick up my four boxes or so filled with wax that I hoped to never see again (though he told me in advance that there was no way I was going to sell that much).

The fair runs for three days: Friday evening, Saturday, and Sunday. The doors open at 7 P.M. on Friday but the early admission cats roll in before that, at four. For the rest of the weekend the hours run 10 A.M.–7 P.M. Twenty dollars gets you an all-access pass including early admission on Friday; á la carte it's five dollars per day.

As you might expect, a lot goes on before the public, even the early birds, gets into the place. The true fanatic dealers will throw their crates on a table, cover that shit with a cloth, and then cruise the hall like some oddly evolved vinyl vulture. And true to that metaphor, a crowd quickly gathers whenever there are two or more predators ripping through the virgin milkcrates, with a lot of furious wheeling and dealing as the cats hope to come up on that find that their brethren overlooked. In my case this was a mint promo copy of Pierre Henry's *Mass for Today* for $10 and an LP by a Quebecois fusion group that had some rap cats salivating when they caught sight of it later in the day.

The first day is short, a Friday evening in which a giddy sense of intoxication at the sheer mass of vinyl pervades the crowd. This can be a dangerous time to shop, as it's too easy to get caught up in some "I've got to get it now,

it'll be gone if I don't snatch it up"-type desperation. While there is obviously some truth to this sentiment, it is also not uncommon to see prices dive on Sunday afternoon. Saturday is a full day and a lot of serious business takes place, with the well-known breeds of heavyweights making their appearances and dropping drool-inducing stacks of cash. Some dealers only show up for one day, and Saturday can be your only chance to catch these folks. By the time Sunday rolls around, the buzz has worn off and things are business-like and less frenzied—until the evening rolls around. Then a new type of desperation sets in, this on the part of the dealers who realize that they are going to have to lug home all this stock they didn't sell. This is obviously prime time to make an offer on some piece that you have been eyeing that was just out of your price range. You also might get lucky and come across a seller who has just drastically marked down a box in order to try and ease the weight on his return trip. This time around I caught a box of classic house records knocked down to $3 each that included the first three releases on Quark Records (Blaze, Exit, and Finchley Road). This was the same crate I was tempted by on the first day at a firm $15 each.

On the whole, it seemed that there were less surprises and "oh shit"-type pieces on display than in the past. At the previous year's WFMU winter fair, I picked up things like the *Yellow Sunshine* LP, Steve Reid's *Nova*, and Leon Haywood's "Cornbread and Buttermilk" 45 for a buck each. This year I was confronted with few such bargains. Maybe as a result of the worldwide increase in beatdigging common knowledge, I saw a lot of "standards" prominently displayed: things like Roy Ayers, Fatback, Axelrod. These were going for high prices, hovering at the Sound Library/A-1/Dusty Groove level that seems to have become the standard. I saw a lot of "golden era" hip-hop being offered too, with the baseline prices around $15.

So how'd I do? Well, I left with a few less records than I came with, and managed to parlay some old Paris and Bill Black Combo records into something a little more fulfilling. I came across many prime examples of the aforementioned record nerd (bad hygiene and no social skills) and a couple of interesting cats. One guy flipping through my offerings paused at an old comp on RCA, *Groupquake*—a psych/blues rock collection notable to me mainly for a Loading Zone song. Too tired and bored to point out that this tune had been used for a Dilated Peoples jam, I let the fella peruse in silence. He continued to stare at the jacket. "There's a nice Loading Zone cut on there," I finally offered, but the dude had already started with "I made a beat off this record…"

"Oh yeah?"

"Yeah. You heard of Dilated Peoples?"

And so, feeling like I was trapped in a loop myself, I was trying to sell the producer known as the Alchemist a record that he had sampled. As the absurdity of it all sunk in I decided it was time to pack up. ●

# Give the Engineer Some

by Andre Torres · photographs by Lance Guerriere

**After hearing the first saxophone on Public Enemy's "Rebel Without a Pause," Scotty Hard realized he could be anything.**

Already discontent with the music scene in Vancouver, Canada, his hometown of nineteen years, he moved to New York City in January 1989 with the intention of getting down with the thriving hip-hop scene. He remembers, "I came into it from that level, seeing it as a new form of music that was really innovative."

Over a decade ago, Brooklyn-based producer/ engineer Scott Harding, aka Scotty Hard, introduced the duo New Kingdom to Gee Street, producing the two critically acclaimed albums that followed. He has since engineered a range of albums, from the Brand New Heavies' *Heavy Rhyme Experience* to Chris Rock's Grammy-winning *Roll with the New*. And at the turn of the century, he coproduced and engineered the first two Blue Note albums for jazz-funk trio Medeski Martin & Wood.

Harding had started his trade rather casually, through years of playing guitar in bands in Vancouver. There's always one guy in the band who knows how to hook up the equipment, and Scotty was that guy. This skill and experience led to some engineering jobs, but the small scene always left him hungry for more. Once in New York, though, Scotty hooked up with friends like Bob Coulter—who was working with Stetsasonic as one of their "Stetgineers"—and got busy. "That was around the time Daddy-O, Prince Paul, and those guys were really hot," Harding recalls. "So they were doing a lot of remixes. When I wasn't working, I'd go hang out with Bob at Green Street [Studios] or Chung King or wherever he was working."

He initially wanted to work at Calliope Studios, the D&D of its day, but at the time they couldn't guarantee him any work. After all, cats like Coulter, Bob Power, and Shane Faber were already putting in much work behind the boards. Through Bob Coulter, however, he got a gig at the legendary Chung King House of Metal. But after not getting paid one too many times, he decided to leave Chung King for the greener pastures of Calliope. It was at Calliope that he got a chance to work with a laundry list of artists from hip-hop's golden age: Stetsasonic, Ultramagnetic MC's, Major Force Posse, De La Soul, the Jungle Brothers, Jazzy Jay, Brand Nubian, Black Sheep, Fat Joe, and the list goes on. "The first session I

ever did," Scotty remembers, "was for Tone Loc for the 'Tone Phone' [a 1-800 number sponsored by MTV]. He came in wearing, like, a white mink coat. It was ill."

But it wasn't all champagne, caviar, and bubble baths. "I started working at Calliope in April of '89, doing like every session. You had no assistant and got paid like ten dollars an hour," says Harding. "You'd get in there, and you'd have to take money from everybody. They were hard-ass about shit back then. If you booked time, you had to put half the money down to reserve your time, then I'd collect [the rest of] the money at the end. So I'm like, 'Okay, well, you owe $192.75, and that's 8.25% sales tax.' I mean you had to figure this all out before the session started, so you're already in this kind of weird position of taking these people's money."

"It was a real ghetto studio," Harding says of Calliope. "Something was always going wrong. I remember one time, I was doing a session with Resident Alien, and the fucking tape machine just started smoking. I mean, smoke just started pouring all out of it!" But out of the smoke came a long-lasting friendship. "That's how I met Prince Paul," he says. "I was working on Resident Alien, which was a group he put together for his label back then with guys he knew from Long Island. A fat guy, a tall, skinny guy, and this little guy with a little arm. They all had green cards that said 'Resident Alien,' and he goes, 'Those three guys look like aliens!' So that's how his mind works."

Collecting money and extinguishing tape machines weren't the only extra work required at sessions, Scotty explains. "You had to either help people make beats or make beats for people." People usually think of the engineer as a studio tech who sets up microphones and records the sessions, but Scotty tells a different story of that era. "In the early days of hip-hop, even the guys who were producers didn't really know how to produce. They didn't know about getting tapes to the studio or overdubbing. They'd just be like, 'Sample this record.' That was back when no one could afford any technology, which is totally different from now, where every motherfucker you know has Pro Tools at home. Back then, you had an eight- or twelve-bit sampler, and a couple of

Scotty Hard at the Magic Shop in Manhattan mixing overdubs for Medeski Martin & Wood.

people might have had an SP-12, because this was even before the SP1200. We had an [Akai] S900, which is like ten seconds of sample memory. And guys would come in, and they'd have a pile of records, and they'd say, 'I want to use this and that,' and you'd loop that up and figure out if it was the tempo they wanted it in. So you ended up being sort of an engineer/programmer, even producing sometimes: 'Hey, maybe you should double that.' Or if something was out of tune, you might mention it. But I learned how to shut up. Sometimes, if something's totally out of tune or fucked up, it's not really your job to do that. But on the other hand, somebody would come back the next week, and they'd be like, 'My man said the vocals was out of tune. Why the fuck you didn't tell me?' So you're damned if you do, damned if you don't."

But, Harding remembers, there were cats who had it together too. "I always thought Mista Lawnge from Black Sheep was really good—besides being a great DJ—but at locking his beats up too." And, Harding adds, "A guy like Prince Paul really knows what he wants, the whole record, and the whole sound of it. He just gives me the track, and I mix it. I mean, Paul was one of the first guys I remember even bringing a disk in."

Sometimes, Harding's extended involvement paid off. Mark the 45 King's remix of pop/R&B singer Lisa Stansfield's hit "All Around the World" would become Harding's most commercially successful session—but not before the record exec passed on 45 King's initial remix. "Because all Mark thought was, 'Yo, I got a beat on it!'" Harding explains. "When he hooked the beat up to it, that was all he thought [a] remix [was]: 'Yo, it's all about that! It's all about the snare drum!' The guy from the record company came in and wanted a full-on remix. I understood what he was talking about. So while we're doing all the edits, Mark is just sitting there smoking, with this little globe radio around his neck. There were a million edits; I used two reels of half-inch for the one song."

## In the early days of hip-hop, even the guys who were producers didn't really know how to produce.

But Mark the 45 King is no fool, and somewhere down the line, it really is all about the snare drum. Scotty has witnessed the evolution of hip-hop's drums over the course of the last decade. "After the DMX and SP-12 era, a lot of people were just using all loops," he says. "All of the early Calliope, Jungle Brothers, [and] De La stuff is all just drum loops. And the earlier you go, the more closely associated they are to all the stuff off the *Ultimate Breaks & Beats* records. Then gradually people started getting other records. Like someone would come in and be like, 'My dad has this Kenny Burrell record and there's a beat on it.' So you'd build everything around a beat."

Scotty continues to drop gems on the golden era: "I know Louie Flores was down with Ultramagnetics—he did a beat on Tim Dog's record. I remember Tim was like, 'I'm putting Louie on; he's from the Bronx.' But Louie did a lot of the edits on the *Ultimate Breaks & Beats*. Sometimes, some of those break records were just one bar, and he would make them into two bars, mainly just so people could use them." Speaking on the longevity of the series, Scotty adds, "Even when we were doing the Ultramag record, which was way after that era, Ced would still be like, 'Let me get the "Pussy Footer" horns.' You know, just using that old shit."

It's that old shit we love too. Scotty has seen it move first-hand from the simple programming of the early beat boxes to the looped beats spurned by the *Ultimate Breaks & Beats* series, to the highly complex arrangements achieved today, not necessarily to his liking. "Most of the stuff you hear on the radio, the drums are programmed. I remember talking to [Dan the] Automator about that. He was like, 'No one's using drum loops anymore.' And I realized, 'Yeah, you're right.' I don't really dig all of this really jiggy, fast stuff that almost has that drum-and-bass sound with all of that really highly programmed drum shit. It's not raw to me. There's nothing raw about that. That's what I like about the whole New York style of it; it's just more ill. I've always been more into that."

That ill, raw sound is what Scotty shoots for when he's behind the boards. "I think it's cooler to emulate records from the '70s instead of emulating records from now. I think that's what I try to do when I engineer shit and make drum sounds, make it sound kinda old. This guy, Garth Richardson, who does stuff like Rage Against the Machine, came into a session I was working on. His dad used to produce the Guess Who, and he's like, 'Wow, my dad used to get drum sounds like that!' And I'm like, 'Alright, thanks, that's a compliment to me.'

## They didn't know about getting tapes to the studio or overdubbing. They'd just be like, "Sample this record."

"I came at it from this musician point of view, always playing in bands. I think that's one reason I've always had good luck with all the jazz records I've made. My brother plays trombone, I used to play in jazz bands, and most of my records are jazz records, so I always knew what instruments sounded like. Whereas a lot of engineers who came up in the '80s, everything was drum machines. But on the other hand, there's guys who made records twenty-five years ago, and if you brought a drum machine into the studio, they'd be freaked out."

It's not only drum machines that freak some engineers out; the mere sight of a session with Wu-Tang Clan is enough for some to head home for the night. Scotty sheds some light on the mystique of the Wu: "I met RZA through Prince Paul from doing the Gravediggaz. We got along pretty well with RZA, and I had done a couple of other late-night remix things. He probably just liked me because I could stay in the studio for fourteen hours, because I'm a fucking idiot! Because those guys would always show up like eight hours late." But Scotty seems to understand the process. "That's his whole style; it's like chaos. His shit is really dope. He's kinda like a conceptual artist in the sense that the idea is more important than the execution." Scotty remembers working on "It's Yourz," one of the more mem-

orable tracks off *Forever*: "I mixed this song like five or six times. I remember RZA really liked it. When we were doing [the remix for Bjork's 'Bachelorette'], he was like, 'Make it like "It's Yourz"!'"

Scotty stays busy these days producing his own tracks on the Brooklyn-based WordSound label. He made his debut solo appearance with his 1999 release *The Return of Kill Dog E*—a dirty blend of banging beats and rumbling bass—and currently produces and plays in Truck Stop, featuring former New Kingdom member Sebastian Laws. Scotty recently completed a breakbeat record with MMW drummer Billy Martin. Regarding his own role in the album, Scotty explains, "As a producer, you're like, *That beat's cool, [but] it'd be great if it wasn't so wet*. So I give it to you dry and wet. But," he adds, "I was also just kind of freestyle mixing it."

In the fickle world of hip-hop, few make it three years much less thirteen. But Scotty Hard has been able to keep himself, and his sound, fresh. Talking about his recording style, he reveals a bit of his secret to longevity: "That's what I do, just sort of get in the mood and do it as a performance, just spontaneously." ⬤

ANDRE TORRES *is Editor-in-Chief of* WAX POETICS.

# All of my gear is totally obsolete. It was when I bought it.

## Akai S950

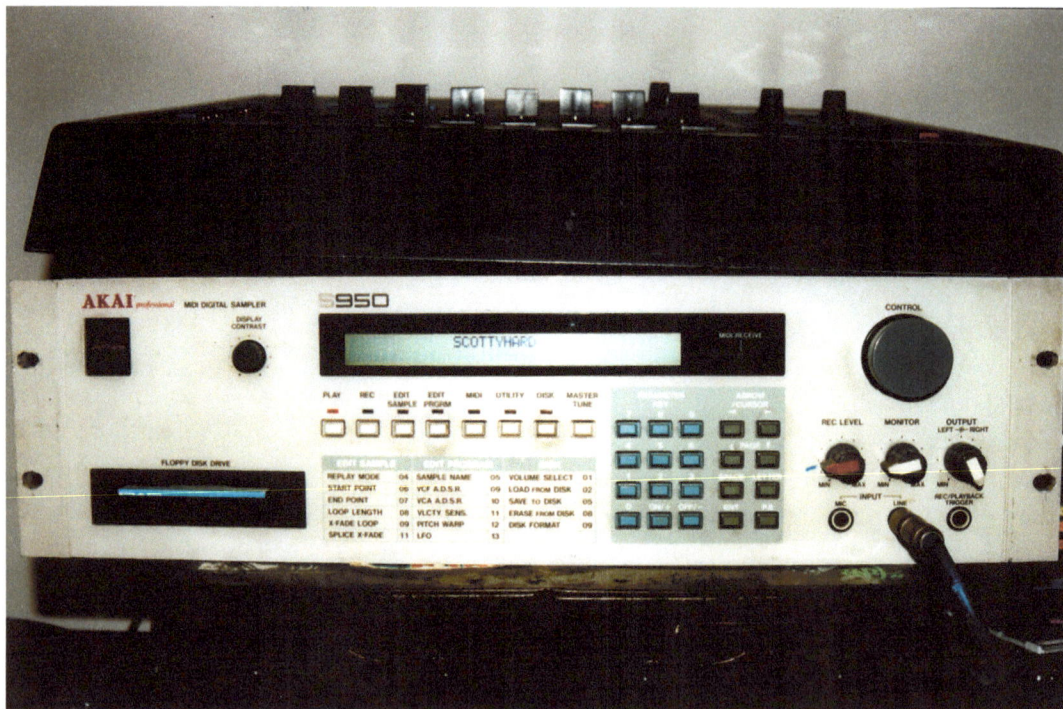

I have the s950, which they don't make anymore; it's 12-bit. I'd say this and the SP12, I use more than anything.

## E-mu SP-12

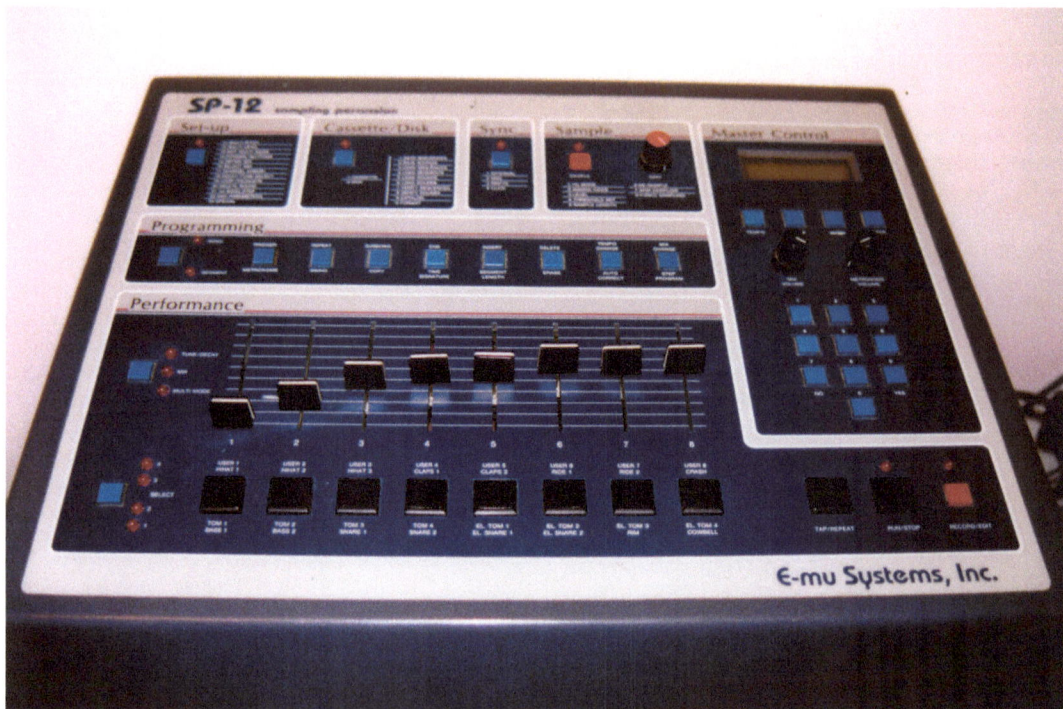

This is the original Calliope 8-bit SP12. Well, one of the originals; they had two. Back in Calliope, this was all we had. We used to run the time code through a delay of one hundred milliseconds, because when you're putting two loops together, it's critical. Once you get it looping within the tempo, you might have had to trigger it a little bit before the kick or a little after. You need to offset the *one* [in the beat count], and everything can be shifted ahead or back. It's not a great way to do things, but that was the essential set up back then.

## Ensoniq ASR-10

I bought this from [Prince] Paul. He couldn't run it off a Zip, but all it was, was that he didn't have the newest operating system.

## Oberheim DMX

I got that off my brother, actually, on one of the New Kingdom tours. I gave him a $100 Canadian for it. I remember I just tied it down with a piece of rope underneath the back seat of the van so it wouldn't shake around on the way from Vancouver back to New York.

## Korg Univox SR 120

This is like the first drum machine, like the kind on [Parliament's] *Chocolate City*. It even comes with a pedal so I can fade it in when I'm doing my duo gigs at the Holiday Inn.

## Yamaha CS60 pre-MIDI synthesizer

It makes a lot of ill, weird sounds. I use it a lot for bass lines, it's fat.

## ARP Omni synthesizer

Yeah, I just got that a few months ago. It's cool, it's got all of these ARP string ensemble sounds, plus all of this synth.

## Allen and Heath mixing board

It's from the late '70s, early '80s. It was designed for these certain Fostex 16-track machines on half-inch tape, which was the beginning of the whole home recording revolution. They had 8-track before that, but a lot of that shit got really popular with the 16-track shit. Then everybody got ADATs and et cetera.

## TASCAM eight-track reel-to-reel recorder

I'm actually mixing an all-percussion record on here next week. Most of the stuff is between five and fifteen tracks, so I can bounce the drums onto the half-inch to thicken them up a bit. It sounds good. And then I can use all of my outputs of Pro Tools, so it's like creating extra outputs. It's cool; it works good.

# Selected Discography

### Production:

**New Kingdom** *Heavy Load* (Gee Street/Island 1993)
**New Kingdom** *Paradise Don't Come Cheap* (Gee Street/Island 1996)
**Medeski Martin & Wood** *Combustication* (Blue Note/Capitol 1998)
**Medeski Martin & Wood** *Last Chance to Dance Trance (perhaps)* (Ryko 1999)
**Medeski Martin & Wood** *The Dropper* (Blue Note/Capitol 2000)
**Sex Mob** *Din of Inequity* (Columbia/Knitting Factory Records 1998)
**DJ Logic** *Project Logic* (RopeADope 2000)
**DJ Logic** *The Anomaly* (RopeADope/Atlantic 2001)
**Material** *Intonarumori* (Axiom/Palm Pictures 1999)
**Jon Spencer Blues Explosion** *XtraAcme USA* (Capitol/Matador 1999)
**Scotty Hard** *The Return of Kill Dog E* (Wordsound 1999)
**Billy Martin** *Illy B Eats, Vol. 1* (Amulet 2001)
**Leon Lamont** *Breakbeat Mechanic* (Wordsound 2000)

### Mixing/Engineering:

**Wu-Tang Clan** *Wu-Tang Forever* (Loud/RCA 1997)
**Wu-Tang Clan** "Can It Be All So Simple" [Remix] *Fresh OST* (RCA 1994)
**Gravediggaz** *6 Feet Deep* (Gee Street/Island 1995)

**Gravediggaz** *The Pick, the Axe and the Shovel* (Gee Street/Island 1997)
**Jungle Brothers** *Raw Deluxe* (Gee Street/V2 1997)
**Chris Rock** *Roll with the New* (Dreamworks 1997)
**Chris Rock** *Bigger and Blacker* (Dreamworks 1999)
**Vernon Reid** *Mistaken Identity* (550/Epic 1996)
**Ultrmagnetic MC's** *Funk Your Head Up* (Mercury 1992)
**Stereo MC's** *Supernatural* (4th & Broadway/Island 1990)
**tomandandy** *Killing Zoe* film score (1994)
**Bjork** "Bachelorette" [RZA Remix] (1997)
**Lifer's Group** *Real Deal* ep (Hollywood Basic 1990)
**Brand New Heavies** *Heavy Rhyme Experience* (Delicious Vinyl 1992)
**Prince Paul, Biz Markie and Chubb Rock** "No Rubbers, No Backstage Pass" *America Is Dying Slowly* (Elektra 1996)
**Boogie Down Productions** *Sex and Violence* (Jive 1992)
**Black Sheep** *A Wolf in Sheep's Clothing* (Mercury 1990)
**Tim Dog** *Penicillin on Wax* (Ruffhouse/Columbia 1991)
**Too Short** "In the Trunk" [DJ Premier Remix] (Jive 1992)
**Cypress Hill** "Latin Lingo" [Prince Paul Mix] (Ruffhouse/Columbia 1991)
**De La Soul** *De La Soul Is Dead* (Tommy Boy 1991)
**Lisa Stansfield** "All Around the World" [45 King Remix] (Arista 1990)
**Handsome Boy Modeling School** *So…How's Your Girl?* (Tommy Boy 1999)

# OLD SCHOOL

**Profile: David Axelrod**
by Tim Schneckloth
from *Down Beat* magazine
December 13, 1977
*reprinted with permission*

Los Angeles is a city that evokes peculiar images in the minds of those who live to the East. To some, L.A. is Plasticland, a place where phoniness and affectation swell to oceanic proportions. To others, it's the model of the future, a town with a vitality and vigor that should be emulated by everyone.

Producer/arranger/composer David Axelrod, however, sees L.A. as a source of inspiration, a continuous stream of hard urban sounds. "Man, you hang around the corner of Normandy and Jefferson and it's no different from any other urban area, I don't care where. A lot of people, all they know is the San Fernando Valley. They think everybody's a surfer. I can't even swim!"

Axelrod's affection for Los Angeles is certainly understandable. It's where he was born and raised; it's where he learned his trade, paid his dues, and draws his current musical schemes. His recent MCA album, *Strange Ladies*, is L.A./urban to the core. How a listener reacts to the record might well correspond to the way he feels about Southern California.

Axelrod is known for his production work with Capitol in the '60s (including a string of Cannonball Adderly releases like *Mercy, Mercy, 74 Miles Away, Country Preacher, Fiddler on the Roof*), as well as his arranging activities. But the desire to compose always came before everything else.

"I met a piano player named Gerald Wiggins and his wife when I was about seventeen. I was kind of like his chauffeur, valet, bodyguard. He taught me how to read music and started explaining intervals and all that. I never really wanted to be a player, I always wanted to be an arranger and composer. I started playing by *writing*."

Axelrod later studied harmony and theory at UCLA and took on some production gigs for Wiggins and others. His involvement with an Elmo Hope/Harold Land session entitled *The Fox* brought him in contact with Cannonball, "Much later," David recalls, "I was sitting in a restaurant, and Ernie Andrews brought Cannonball over. Cannonball's exact words were, 'Aha, *The Fox*! I knew our paths would cross again someday.'

"A few years went by and I was with Capitol. They signed Cannonball and asked him who he wanted for a producer. He said, 'Get me Axe!' and we were together for twelve years."

During his tenure at Capitol, Axelrod took a few days off to work on a rather bizarre 1967 project at Warner Brothers. It was *Mass in F Minor* by the Electric Prunes, a record that met with wildly mixed criticism (a major news magazine did a story on the record, referring to it as a breakthrough album; some others were less enthusiastic). "I composed and arranged it," Axelrod says. "The Electric Prunes were not on it. They couldn't read. I had all the charts laid out for them, and we started doing the date. In a three-hour date, I think we cut four bars of music. I looked at Dave Hassinger, the producer, and said, "We're *never* going to do this thing. It'll be a career. We'll be in the studio forty years from now.' So we got studio guys.

"At the time, it was a fairly revolutionary thing for rock, because it had jazz solos on it. The distortion of the guitars was actually part of the orchestration. There's no problem saying it now, but I like it."

As a result of this experience, Axelrod got his first record date under his own name at Capitol. Now, at MCA, David enjoys full artistic control of his projects and a comfortable working relationship with MCA president Mike Maitland.

What Axelrod has done for the label so far reflects varied influences, but the actual sources are nebulous. "I'm just not conscious of them. You're always drawing on things that you hear. I hate the idea of pigeonholing music. What I do is *urban*. I was born in the city. The first time I ever saw a forest was on the way to the Monterey Jazz Festival in '61.

"LeRoi Jones said a very good thing: 'Environment is total.' It's not just scenery, It's social, cultural, and physical. If anything, that's the kind of music I think I write.

"I try to listen to everything that I possibly can. I listen to a lot of classical music, a lot of jazz, a lot of rock. I like the Who, Earth Wind & Fire, Tower of Power. I love Stanley Clarke. And anything Miles does, *anything*.

"Gil Evans is so subtle with everything. You have to listen to him very closely. All of a sudden you'll hear something that's been there all the time, and you'll say, 'Where did that come from?' Beautiful arranger. He was an influence, so was Duke.

"During the '50s I was totally wrapped up in jazz. We would listen to Blakey and everything that came out of New York. When Presley came out, I kept hearing his name for about six months, but I honestly didn't know who he was. I had never heard an Elvis Presley record. But I had listened to Louis Jordan, Amos Milburn, Roy Milton—that was *my* rock and roll.

"In the '60s, with the Beatles and everything, I have to admit it was my children that hipped me to these things. I had a manager that was handling a lot of English groups, and the group Traffic knocked me out. And *they* had been knocked out by an album I had done called *Songs of Innocence*."

By and large, Axelrod is happy with the state of contemporary music today. "I think it's great, because it gives you a tremendous amount of freedom. I feel that the consumer is a lot more open than the media. The media don't know what the consumer can absorb and is willing to consume and take and buy.

"Radio is probably five years behind what the buyer is buying. The big Top 40 stations are actually being patronizing to their listeners. They don't take into consideration that the listener is probably more mature than the program director.

"A good example is Weather Report or the Crusaders. *Heavy Weather* went high on the charts, but the Top 40 stations never played it. Eventually, that will come back to haunt them."

Despite such frustrations, Axelrod continues to write in and about L.A., adjusting his working schedule to whatever project he is working on. "Recently, I did the score for a movie called, ironically, *Cannonball* with David Carradine. It was about car racing and all that. I had only two weeks to write it, so this was a situation where I did have a schedule. I started every day at ten and quit at six. That was a job; I knew I had to make the music. I sat down every day at the piano, ran the reels off, corrected the timing and wrote the music."

David is enamored of the synthesizer, even though he doesn't think of himself as much of an instrumentalist. "I can't chord on the keyboard. I had a very bad accident a few years back that smashed up three fingers. So the synthesizer was made for me. I can work with single notes on my right hand. On this particular album, though, I didn't use synthesizer because I just didn't *hear* it."

But irregardless [*sic*] of the means of expression, Axelrod continues to try to get a tonal equivalent of his urban perceptions. "There's a lot of tension in music. Cannon used to say, 'There's a lot of violence in music.' Maybe it's subconscious thing. You may listen to it and think it's pretentious. But if there's one thing I'm not, it's pretentious." ◗

# The Power of Soul
# Idris Muhammad

Interview by Eothen Alapatt
Photos by Duane Michals for the 1974
KUDU release *Power of Soul*

I met Idris through Jimmy Lewis. I needed a drummer. We'd had a drummer on *Hair* when we were doing it downtown. He'd gone out of town, but he wasn't quite what we wanted anyway. So I asked Jimmy, "Who should we get?" He said, "Idris." He had worked with Idris as a sessioner and in the King Curtis Band. I think I had Idris come play with us, but it may have been that we went straight into rehearsals. He was great, right from the start. He had a great, strong beat. And he played in the right style. He actually was a jazz drummer but when he heard the music for *Hair* he didn't go the wrong way. He went right with it. He stayed in the band for four and a half years. He created a book of drumming, for when he missed the show. [Idris's subs] had to try to do what he did, and none of them could. He was so powerful; it was unbelievable! After he played that show for about a year, I said, "We've got to record this band; they're so good!" And then we did the *First Natural Hair Band* LP. "Ripped Open by Metal Explosions" is probably the most funky outing on the record but Idris had a lot of moments in the show that were really terrific. Towards the end of the show it goes into pure rhythm for about twenty minutes. Idris just kept it up, it was great. From one song to the other, with lots of breaks and interesting stuff. I used Idris for other projects, like the *Woman Is Sweeter* LP, and lots of demos. I used his wife Sakinah too. We all had a close relationship. But after the show closed, he moved out. He was traveling, playing with jazz groups and such. So I started with Bernard [Purdie] again. I'd kept in touch with him anyway during that time. For certain things, I used Bernard. The two are just different. Bernard is very sharp, you know. He plays a lot of interesting rhythms. Idris concentrates not so much on rhythm as on the beat—the actual four beats in the bar. And he generates a terrific momentum, like a train going down a hill. I don't know anyone who does that better than Idris. And in a show, it's overwhelming. By the end of the show the audience is breathless because of this unbelievable drumming. They didn't know it, but I knew that's what it was.

—Galt MacDermot, as told to Eothen Alapatt, 4/8/01

*The following interview originally aired on the WRVU 91.1 FM radio show "Origins of Hip-Hop" in Nashville, Tennessee in the spring of 1999.*

### Where were you born?

New Orleans—that's my home. Sixty-one years have gone by so fast I'm shocked. I was born Leo Morris. My father's family originated from Nigeria and my mother was French. When I came into the family, there were seven of us. My three brothers, and one of my sisters, were drummers. The first day I went in to school, the teacher gave me a drum. She said, "Here's another Morris; give him a drum!" I went home with this drum and, man, my mother was mad! She said, "Oh shit, not another one! I got to buy khaki pants, a white shirt, a yellow tie, and a blue jacket so he can be in the band!"

### Well, you had to follow the Morris's musical dynasty!

See, I was just a kid trying to play cowboys and Indians. I wanted cap pistols! But it was already written that this was going to happen. I lived in a neighborhood that was full of musicians and schoolteachers. Any day, you could hear music just walking the streets—somebody playing, rehearsing. Or you'd hear these marching bands in the streets.

### Of course. Any introductory jazz textbook talks about the all-encompassing nature of music in New Orleans.

Because of the drums in the house, I would run around and hit the cymbals in the backyard. I liked music; it was in the house all the time. I think my attention focused when the bands in the neighborhood would play in the streets. I lived near two bars, a club, and a restaurant. The bands would do what we called a "dry run." They'd start rehearsing in a guy's house, then they'd come out of the house and go down the street, and people would follow them right into a bar. It was spontaneous. You understand? Someone would say, "Get the band a drink!" and then they'd move on to the next bar. This was my beginning in music, because the music was there. My thing was the bass drum. I used to hear this *boom boom boom* and I'd run out the house and dance underneath the bass drum player. I can still remember the guy with the bass drum saying "Move your ass from under this drum or I'll hit you with this mallet!" I was walking between the bass drum player and the snare drum player.

### An important point regarding the precision that New Orleans's drummers embody—in marching bands, the drum kit had to be separated.

Well, you had a guy that played the bass drum with a cymbal at the top that he played with a coat hanger attached to a broomstick. That was the hi-hat. And then you had the snare drum player. These were bands that would play for funerals—or for any occasion. Back in those days you'd go to the same school from start to grade twelve. So my first professor was my musical director all the way through high school. And him and my older brother, "Weedy" Morris, were the first two Black musicians in Louisiana to be inducted into the Navy Band. My brother was the snare drum player, and my professor played the bass drum. While they were in the service, Weedy said, "When you get out, look for my brother and them." All of the drummers I met coming up in New Orleans knew him.

### What led to your professional start?

It was one Mardi Gras day, and I was eight or nine. A guy came by the house looking for drummers. He asked for me—these old Dixieland musicians wanted me! They begged my mother; they said they'd take care of me. I played on the back of a flatbed truck. They set up three or four beer cases for me to sit on and gave me a kick drum, snare, and a cymbal. I knew all the songs, so I started playing. I was in the parade, and the kids from school saw me. One thing I'll never forget, there was this girl from school I was trying to talk to, but she would never look at me. She would come to school every day, all pressed and ironed. This day she saw me, and she said, "Hey, Leo!" I was playing drums in the parade! Then they slipped me a little wine, and at the end they were passing this money out: I got two fives. I said, "You get paid for this?" The man said, "Yeah!" That was it. That's when I decided I would be a musician. See, in those days going to the movies cost twelve cents. And from then on, it was a different story with that girl. You know what I mean? I went home, gave my mom five dollars, and then I took all my buddies to the movies. I said, "Mom, I'm going to be a musician."

### Did your parents recognize your nascent talent?

One day, my father told my mother, "Tell Sydney to stop playing!" Sydney was my older brother. My father had just come home from work and he wanted to smoke his pipe and read the paper. So my mother went around back and saw me playing the drums. She didn't say anything and left. My father said, "Tell the kid to stop it with that noise!" She said, "You go tell him!" Well, he went back there, saw it was me, and he was shocked! He said that he thought it was my older brother. He had no idea!

### You never had any formal training?

No. See, I'm a natural drummer. I'm a drummer that inherited the drums from my family. And my father was a banjo player. He played with Louis Armstrong back in the days. But we had so many kids that he became an interior decorator to support us. He couldn't do it just playing music. But he used to sing to us all of these songs—standards. My mother would be cooking, and we were all fooling around, so he'd take us alongside him and sing us these songs. From my father, I inherited a musical ability. That's where the musical part of my drumming comes from. See, my drumming is different from the rest of the drummers, 'cause I'm a musical drummer. I play the musical part of the song. I inherited a gift from the Creator. I can do things with the drums that no other drummer I know can do.

### So when did you really start gigging?

That's so interesting! I started going to my brother's gigs and waiting till he decided I could play a song with the band—maybe the last song of the night. The Nevilles are my family. We lived in the same neighborhood. So Aaron and I used to play gigs at Tulane and LSU with our music professor. We'd also go to see Arthur Neville's band, which at that time was called the Hawkettes.

**The Hawkettes would later become the Meters.**

Well, the band would play at the YMCA. We would go to the dance, and then I would sit in with the band, and Aaron would sit in with his brother. At the time, both John Boudreux and Smokey Johnson were drumming for the Hawkettes. I knew them both. They would come to my house to practice on my drum set, 'cause my mother had bought me a tape recorder. They'd practice and listen to themselves on the tape recorder. Smokey would play like Art Blakey. John would play like Max Roach. I'd listen to them for hours. Next thing you know, I could play what they both played. We were all Scorpios, all born in the same month. This started me practicing different things with the drums. Then John went on the road with Eddie Bo; the Hawkettes needed a drummer. So Arthur's father, who was their manager, said, "Go around the corner and get Leo." They said, "Well, he could play with us, but he doesn't have a set of drums!" I'm like fourteen years old. So my mother made Sydney lend me his drums. We traveled—Bogalusa, Shreveport, Baton Rouge. We had four

thing I was making money so fast! Man, when I was living at home I was wearing clothes tailor-made on Rampart Street. I was clean!

**What led you out of New Orleans?**

Fate came through in this area. I came back with Arthur Neville, and the band wasn't working. I met this guy Joe Jones. We had a hit record, so I went on the road with him. Then I met Dee Clarke and Jerry Butler. They flipped over my drum playing! Once I was with Joe at a restaurant, and he told me Sam Cooke was sitting in the dining room. Joe told me Sam was complaining about his drummer. See, Joe had the gift of gab. He said, "I've been talking with him, and I want you to meet him." So we went over to his table, and Sam asked me to sit down. He asked if I knew his songs, I said, "Yeah." He started singing, and I started playing on the table. He hired me right there. He said, "Come to the Municipal Auditorium and play with me tonight." When he went on, I went on. I played that show without a rehearsal. And nailed it! I left town with

gigs that weekend. So I'm playing with the band, and the father said, "He knows all our music!" When I came back, my brother asked me if I wanted to buy his drums. See, he was moonlighting as a delivery boy for the corner drugstore. The chemist was a drummer and his wife told him she'd leave him if he hit another note! He wanted to sell my brother his drums. My brother said, "Leo, you want my drums? Give me $15." His drums were Ludwig, wooden drums. Now I had my own set of drums. That was forty-seven years ago. I shot straight up during those years. At home, I played with Eddie Bo, Earl King, and Lloyd Price. I went on the road with Arthur in 1957 with Larry Williams. We recorded some good records. Man, I was recording at fifteen years old!

**Were you making good money?**

My father asked me what I would do for a living. I said, "I'm going to play the drums, pop!" Once I started this

Sam Cooke. He brought me to New York. My first trip to New York, and I was his personal drummer, man.

**But you didn't stay in New York.**

No, I came back to New Orleans, and another guy from New Orleans took my gig with Sam. I went back out with Joe Jones. But Maxine Brown took me to New York again. We were opening at the Apollo Theater. Jerry Butler was the star on the bill. But I was playing with Maxine Brown. She bought me my first brand-new set of drums. Jerry said [of our performance], "Damn, man, he got that burning for her. Maybe I can get that for me." So I played for him on the same show! I made a whole lot of money. I went to Chicago and Curtis Mayfield started playing the guitar. I ended up being Jerry's musical director. Then I left Jerry and went with Curtis.

**So how did you end up playing jazz again?**

My wife, who was the lead singer with the Crystals, was living in New York. I was living in Chicago. I decided I would come to New York to be with her. When I got there, I had no gig, so I went to the Apollo Theater. I met with Reuben Phillips, the Apollo's bandleader, and let him know I was in town. He fired the drummer in the Apollo band and hired me! So I was in the band for about a year and a half. As I worked there, I was playing around town, sitting in with this group and that group. One day, I went down to this club called the Five Spot, and I sat in with Rashaan Roland Kirk. When I finished, this guy came up to me and said I sounded good—could I do a concert with him? His name was Kenny Dorham. So now I'm playing a concert at Town Hall with Kenny Dorham's band, Freddie Hubbard's band, and Lee Morgan's band. So I met all of these jazz musicians.

**And you went on to infuse New York jazz with the diverse influences you picked up in New Orleans in your fledgling years.**

I'm a natural drummer. I have some special qualities that came from the Creator which allow me to play all kinds of music. In New Orleans, you had to play for all different kinds of people. You played bar mitzvahs, you played at the universities, you played jazz, you played the street music, Latin music. I didn't know that my repertoire for music was so vast until I came to New York.

**And jazz was changing from an intellectual music that had to be "appreciated" to a danceable, fun music again.**

Right. The straightahead bebop took a step backwards to the music that was coming up that had a beat to it. I didn't know it at the time, but I was setting the trend for this music. I met Lou Donaldson at Birdland on 52nd Street. I was coming up the stairs, he was coming down the stairs. Bill Hartman, a trumpet player, said, "Hey Lou, that's the little drummer I was telling you about." Lou said, "Hey you, can you swing?" I said, "Yeah." He said, "You working this weekend? Gimme your number." And he called me. I went to Baltimore, and we played a gig. During the first tune we played, he turned around and told Bill, "We got ourselves a drummer!" Within two weeks, I'm in the studio recording with Lou for Blue Note. My first record for Blue Note was *Alligator Bogaloo*. It was an instant hit. Oh, man, next thing you know Blue Note is calling me to record with George Benson, Lee Morgan, Stanley Turrentine. All of these guys.

**Not surprisingly. You were a hit maker.**

Yeah, my track record for R&B had already been set down. I had made hit records with the Impressions. I have a gift, man, that I can tune into your music. I can make your music better than what you thought you wrote. I had no idea I was doing this. But next thing you know, I'm record-ing with all these guys. I'm doing so well that I'm shocked. Everybody's saying, "This Leo Morris is a bad cat." I met Eric Gale, Chuck Rainey, Ralph McDonald. These were the session guys that were doing the R&B and funk stuff in New York. They latched into me, got me doing dates.

**What were those Prestige and Blue Note dates like?**

We'd just go to Rudy Van Gelder's studio and run through the song a few times. They might give me chord changes, but they never gave me no notes, 'cause they relied on me to play something to make the song happen.

**You and Bernard Purdie supplied the backbeat to the entire soul-jazz movement!**

[*laughs*] But Bernard could never play the drums that I played. He is a great drummer with his own style. But guys learned how to play the drums from me. There were things I was doing with the drums that guys took and made their trademark.

**Like what?**

That hi-hat thing that Bernard does. That *shoop shoop shoop*. This is something that I created. I was the drummer with Galt MacDermot for *Hair*. We played onstage with the actors, on the back of a flatbed truck. My drum set was set near the cab of the truck. I could only have one ride cymbal and the hi-hat. So I played all of this music off of the hi-hat, and I accented off the ride cymbal. After a year and a half I became sick, so they sent in a sub to play for me, and it was a disaster! After I came back, Galt made me get a book written up. Eventually, I had nine drummers subbing for me. This started with Bernard Purdie, Billy Cobham, Alphonse Mouzon. All these guys were subbing for me, 'cause this was the hottest musical on Broadway. So I'd created this thing off the hi-hat. Bernard comes by and looks at the book and says, "I can't play this shit, Idris!" And he leaves. Next time I heard that thing was on Aretha Franklin's "Spanish Harlem." I saw Bernard, he said, "Did you hear what I stole from you? This hi-hat lick." So guys were taking things from my drum playing and incorporating it into their style of drum playing.

**And a lot of musicians were influenced by *Hair*.**

I met Miles Davis two years before he died. We were playing a gig and he asked me who I was playing with. He said, "Idris, you should get a band together and play some of that funky shit I heard you play in *Hair*. When I saw *Hair*, I changed my whole band. I knew there was money in that kind of music."

**Wow, right around the time of *Bitches Brew*.**

That's right! He changed everything to electric.

**And got Jack DeJohnette to play funky rhythms— like you played. What do you know about the hip-hop movement?**

They hear these beats and they take a part of it and sample them. I wasn't hip to it till my son Idris Jr. showed me what these guys were doing. I've met some hip-hop musicians. These guys said that they could get into the stuff I did really fast 'cause it's so clean, so natural—but funky.

**Your drum beat is instrumental to '90s hip-hop production.**

That's the nucleus of the music, the beat. If they don't have the beat how can the rappers do their thing right? The rappers have told me that with my drumbeat, the lyrics go right.

**On top of that, you had such a bangin' sound on your kit.**

I have a unique way of tuning my drums. I learned this as a youngster, and at Rudy's [studio] on the [mixing] board. Rudy took my drum playing and put it up front and put all of the other instruments around it. So when you first hear my record, you hear the drum. On all of these guys' records! I learned to get my drum sound in the studio. So if I just meet an engineer, I know how to explain what I'm going for, so he and I will have a good rapport.

**There's nothing worse than having a great drummer paired with a bad engineer. How about your equipment itself?**

Well, there's a funny story about that. Art Blakey heard me play at the Five Spot the night after someone stole my cymbal bag. I was using cymbals some guy brought in, and he said, "Son, you sound real great but those pot covers you're playing on don't do you no justice!" He said, "I'll be back after you get off, and I got something at the house I think I can give you." So I hung out with him for two and a half days before I got back to my apartment. I ended up with the cymbals that I made all of the records that you're talking about on. I've had those cymbals for thirty-two years. I'm playing with them right now.

**Wow! How do you feel about the appropriation of your music by the hip-hop generation?**

I think it's a great music, man; look at the record sales. These guys sell so many records that they only have to have one hit.

**But how do you feel about the movement artistically?**

Yeah, I like it, 'cause it's another phase of the music.

**Even though hip-hop musicians appropriate your music? And you're not necessarily getting paid for it?**

It don't really belong to me, man; I'm only the creator. If you take something I create, and you do something with it, then someone else will take it and move it to another stage. And this is what happened with hip-hop. This is in my aura. I'm doing stuff for people to put out there so people can grab it. The gift the Creator has given me, I can't be selfish with. If I keep it in my pocket, it's not going to go anyplace. It doesn't matter if a guy stole from me. I'd say, "Well, what did you do? Okay, let me show you this." This is how I live.

**That's a very humble attitude.**

I watched people. I used to travel with the rock-and-roll shows. I watched stars. I got to the point where I had *Turn This Mother Out* and it frightened me. I had a big record. I was opening for the Jackson 5, but the saddest point in my life was being a star and being in the dressing room by myself. And then the most sad thing was that the band was on the bandstand, and I had to wait for the police to escort me to the stage. I'm by myself. I'm used to being with the band. I was a sad dude, man.

**I wish more people were as open-minded about their music as you are.**

Well, you see, man, it don't belong to us. Secretly, whatever you have is gonna come out anyhow. If you think you are hiding something—you have a private vault that you have stuff in—when you leave this world your wife is going to open it up and sell everything. She's gonna sell everything in that vault! It's gonna come out anyway. So why not be free with it while you're here and share it with other people? 'Cause it don't belong to you. ◉

Eothen Alapatt *likes cats and old records. Sometimes he gets the two confused. When he's not managing Stones Throw Records, he's either wasting time haggling with record dealers or doing some serious research. The Idris Muhammad piece in this issue is a result of the latter. He's also a Cancer, and he has brown eyes.*

# Idris Muhammad Selected Discography

*Black Rhythm Revolution!* (Prestige 1970)
*Peace and Rhythm (Salam Wa Nagama)* (Prestige 1971)
*Power of Soul* (Kudu 1974)
*House of the Rising Sun* (Kudu 1975)
*Turn This Mutha Out* (Kudu 1977)
*Boogie to the Top* (Kudu 1978)
*You Aint No Friend of Mine* (Fantasy 1978)
*Fox Huntin'* (Fantasy 1979)
*Make It Count* (Fantasy 1980)
*Kabsha* (Theresa 1980)
*My Turn* (Lipstick 1993)
*Right Now* (Cannonball 1998)

Stefan Pelzl's Juju & Idris Muhammad *Tales of Sisyphos* (RST 1996)

Nat Adderley *Calling Out Loud* (A&M/CTI 1968)
Gene Ammons *Black Cat* (Prestige 1970)
Gene Ammons *My Way* (Prestige 1970)
Gene Ammons with Sonny Stitt *You Talk That Talk* (Prestige 1971)
Amiri Baraka *It's Nation Time* (Black Forum 1972)
George Benson *Other Side of Abbey Road* (CTI 1970)
Walter Bishop, Jr. *Coral Keys* (Black Jazz 1971)
Luiz Bonfá *Jacaranda* (Ranwood 1973)
Rusty Bryant *Soul Liberation* (Prestige 1970)
Rusty Bryant *Fire Eater* (Prestige 1971)
Rusty Bryant *Wildfire* (Prestige 1971)
Rusty Bryant *Friday Night Funk for Saturday Night Brothers* (Prestige 1973)
Gary Chandler *Outlook* (Eastbound 1972)
Merry Clayton *Keep Your Eye on the Sparrow* (Ode 1975)
Hank Crawford *Help Me Make It Through the Night* (Kudu 1972)
Hank Crawford *Wildflower* (CTI 1973)
Hank Crawford *Don't You Worry 'Bout a Thing* (CTI 1974)
Paul Desmond *Summertime* (CTI 1968)
Lou Donaldson *Alligator Bogaloo* (Blue Note 1967)
Lou Donaldson *Mr. Shing-A-Ling* (Blue Note 1967)
Lou Donaldson *Midnight Creeper* (Blue Note 1968)
Lou Donaldson *Say It Loud!* (Blue Note 1968)
Lou Donaldson *Everything I Play Is Funky* (Blue Note 1969)
Lou Donaldson *Hot Dog* (Blue Note 1969)
Lou Donaldson *Pretty Things* (Blue Note 1970)
Lou Donaldson *Cosmos* (Blue Note 1971)
Lou Donaldson *Sassy Soul Strut* (Blue Note 1973) [uncredited]
Lou Donaldson *Scorpion: Live at the Cadillac Club* (Blue Note 1995)
Charles Earland *Black Talk!* (Prestige 1969)
Pee Wee Ellis *Home in the Country* (Savoy 1976)
Fania All-Stars *Social Change* (Fania 1981)
Roberta Flack *Feel Like Makin' Love* (Atlantic 1975)
Dean Fraser *Big Up!* (Island 1998)
Ceasar Frazier *Hail Ceasar!* (Eastbound 1972)
Eric Gale *Forecast* (Kudu 1973)
Grant Green *Carryin' On* (Blue Note 1969)
Grant Green *Alive!* (Blue Note 1970)
Grant Green *Green Is Beautiful* (Blue Note 1970)
Grant Green *Visions* (Blue Note 1971)
Gene Harris and the Three Sounds *Self-Titled* (Blue Note 1971)
Andrew Hill *Previously Unreleased Session* [*Grass Roots* CD] (Blue Note 1969)

Richard "Groove" Holmes *Good Vibrations* (Muse 1977)
Richard "Groove" Holmes *Shippin' Out* (Muse 1978)
Freddie Hubbard *New Colors* (Hip Bop 2001)
Bobbi Humphrey *Flute In* (Blue Note 1971)
J & K *Betwixt & Between* (A&M/CTI 1969)
Willis "Gator Tail" Jackson *Bar Wars* (Muse 1977)
Willis "Gator Tail" Jackson *Single Action* (Muse 1978)
Bob James *One* (CTI 1974)
Bob James *Touchdown* (Columbia 1978)
Bob James *Lucky Seven* (Columbia 1979)
Bob James *All Around the Town* (Columbia 1981)
Rodney Jones *Soul Manifesto* (Blue Note 2001)
Charles Kynard *Wa-Tu-Wa-Zui* (Prestige 1970)
Ron Levy *Zim Zam Zoom: Acid Blues on B-3* (Bullseye Blues 1996)
Ron Levy's Wild Kingdom *Greaze Is What's Good* (Cannonball 1998)
Wilbert Longmire *Champagne* (CBS 1979)
Harold Mabern *Wailin'* (Prestige 1969)
Harold Mabern *Greasy Kid Stuff!* (Prestige 1970)
Galt MacDermot *Woman Is Sweeter* (Kilmarnock 1969)
Galt MacDermot *Haircuts* (Kilmarnock 1969)
Galt MacDermot's First Natural Hair Band *Self-Titled* (United Artists 1970)
Galt MacDermot *Up From the Basement* (Kilmarnock 2000)
Bill Mason *Gettin' Off* (Eastbound 1972)
David "Fathead" Newman *Concrete Jungle* (Prestige 1976)
David "Fathead" Newman *Keep the Dream Alive* (Prestige 1977)
Don Patterson *Why Not* (Muse 1978)
Houston Person *Person to Person* (Prestige 1970)
Houston Person *Real Thing* (Eastbound 1973)
Pharoah Sanders *Jewels of Thought* (Impulse! 1969)
Pharoah Sanders *Journey to the One* (Theresa 1980)
Shirley Scott *Lean On Me* (Cadet 1972)
Horace Silver *That Healin' Feelin'* (Blue Note 1970)
Lonnie Smith *Turning Point* (Blue Note 1969)
Melvin Sparks *Sparks!* (Prestige 1970)
Melvin Sparks *Spark Plug* (Prestige 1971)
Melvin Sparks *Akilah* (Prestige 1973)
Melvin Sparks *Texas Twister* (Eastbound 1973)
Melvin Sparks *'75* (Westbound 1975) [uncredited]
Leon Spencer *Sneak Preview* (Prestige 1970)
Leon Spencer *Louisiana Slim* (Prestige 1971)
Leon Spencer *Where I'm Coming From* (Prestige 1972)
Leon Spencer *Bad Walking Woman* (Prestige 1972)
Sonny Stitt *Turn It On* (Prestige 1971)
Sonny Stitt *Black Vibrations* (Prestige 1971)
Sonny Stitt *Goin' Down Slow* (Prestige 1972)
Fats Theus *Black Out* (CTI 1970)
Stanley Turrentine *Common Touch* (Blue Note 1968)
Stanley Turrentine *Don't Mess with Mister T.* (CTI 1973)
Stanley Turrentine *The Man with the Sad Face* (Fantasy 1976)
Grover Washington, Jr. *Inner City Blues* (Kudu 1971)
Grover Washington, Jr. *Soul Box* (Kudu 1973)
Reuben Wilson *Love Bug* (Blue Note 1969)
Various Artists *Hair (The Original Broadway Cast Recording)* (RCA 1968)
Various Artists *The Lost Grooves* (Blue Note 1995)
Various Artists *Blue Note Rare Grooves* (Blue Note 1996)

Steve Kader and Oliver Wang contributed
to the following pictorial discography.

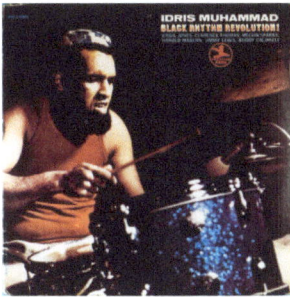

Idris Muhammad
*Black Rhythm Revolution!*

Idris Muhammad
*Peace and Rhythm*

Idris Muhammad
*Power of Soul*

Idris Muhammad
*House of the Rising Sun*

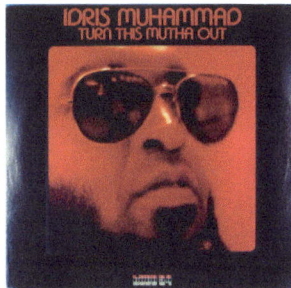

Idris Muhammad
*Turn This Mutha Out*

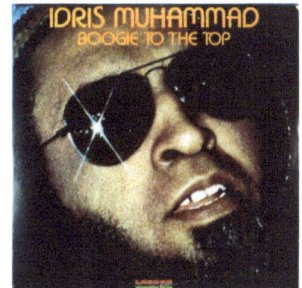

Idris Muhammad
*Boogie to the Top*

Idris Muhammad
*Fox Huntin'*

Nat Adderley
*Calling Out Loud*

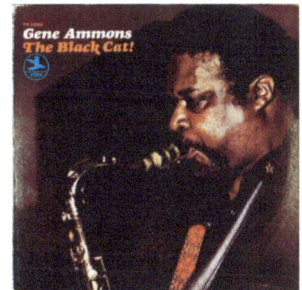

Gene Ammons
*Black Cat*

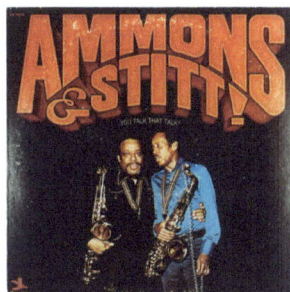

Gene Ammons w/ Sonny Stitt
*You Talk That Talk*

George Benson
*Other Side of Abbey Road*

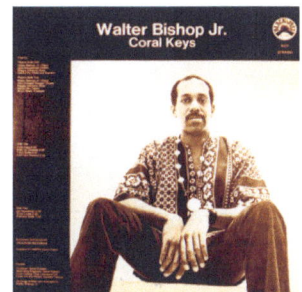

Walter Bishop, Jr.
*Coral Keys*

Luiz Bonfá
*Jacaranda*

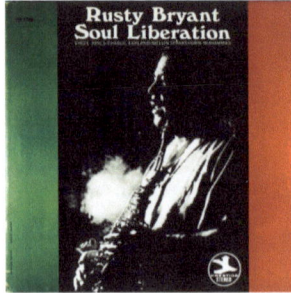

Rusty Bryant
*Soul Liberation*

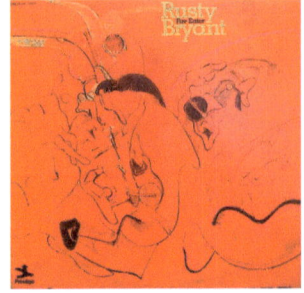

Rusty Bryant
*Fire Eater*

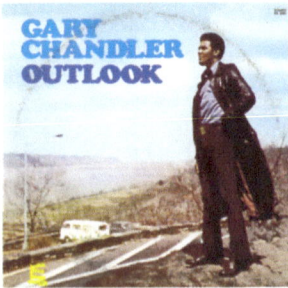

Gary Chandler
*Outlook*

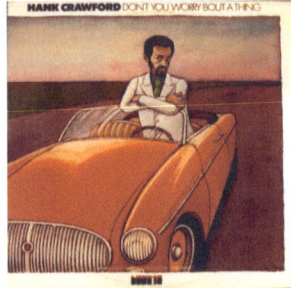

Hank Crawford
*Don't You Worry 'Bout a Thing*

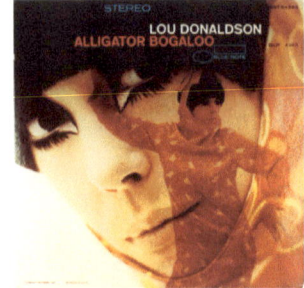

Lou Donaldson
*Alligator Bogaloo*

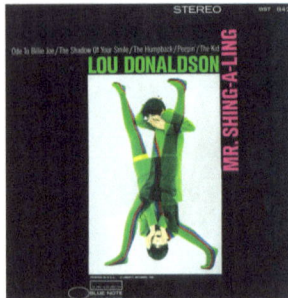

Lou Donaldson
*Mr. Shing-a-Ling*

Lou Donaldson
*Everything I Play Is Funky*

Lou Donaldson
*Hot Dog*

Lou Donaldson
*Pretty Things*

Lou Donaldson
*Cosmos*

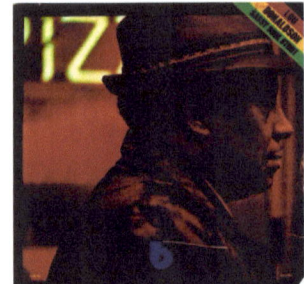

Lou Donaldson
*Sassy Soul Strut*

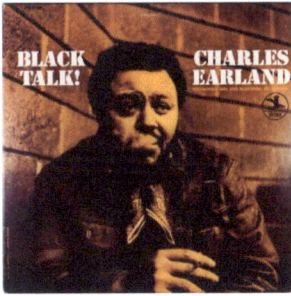

Charles Earland
*Black Talk!*

Roberta Flack
*Feel Like Makin' Love*

Ceasar Frazier
*Hail Ceasar!*

Eric Gale
*Forecast*

Grant Green
*Carryin' On*

Grant Green
*Alive!*

Grant Green
*Green Is Beautiful*

Grant Green
*Visions*

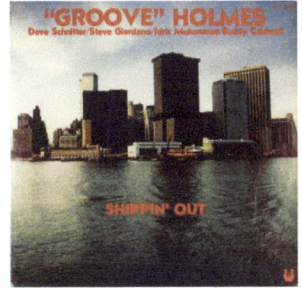

Richard "Groove" Holmes
*Shippin' Out*

Bobbi Humphrey
*Flute In*

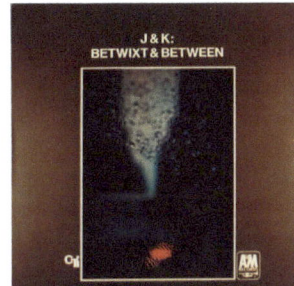

J & K
*Betwixt & Between*

Bob James
*One*

Bob James
*All Around the Town*

Charles Kynard
*Wa-Tu-Wa-Zui*

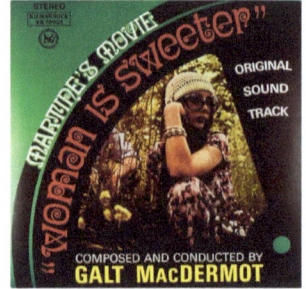

Galt MacDermot
*Woman Is Sweeter*

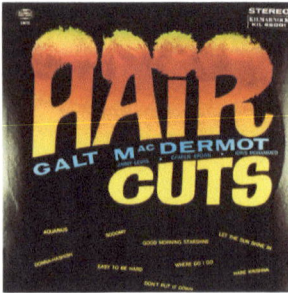

Galt MacDermot
*Hair Cuts*

*Galt MacDermot's First Natural Hair Band*

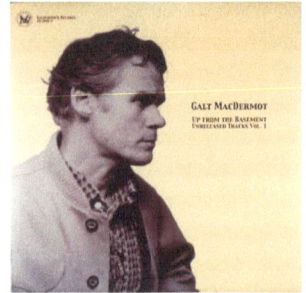

Galt MacDermot
*Up From the Basement*

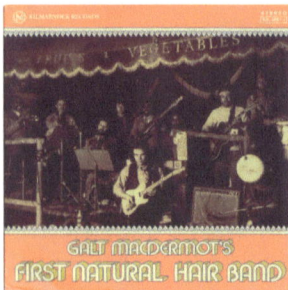

Galt MacDermot
*"Ripped Open by Metal Explosions" 7-inch*

Bill Mason
*Gettin' Off*

David "Fathead" Newman
*Concrete Jungle*

David "Fathead" Newman
*Keep the Dream Alive*

Pharoah Sanders
*Jewels of Thought*

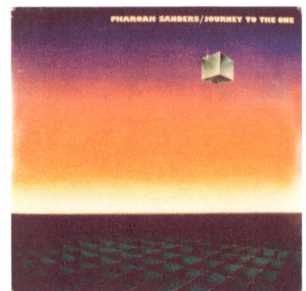

Pharoah Sanders
*Journey to the One*

Shirley Scott
*Lean On Me*

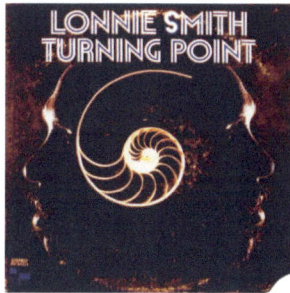

Lonnie Smith
*Turning Point*

Melvin Sparks
*Spark Plug*

Melvin Sparks
*Akilah*

Melvin Sparks
*'75*

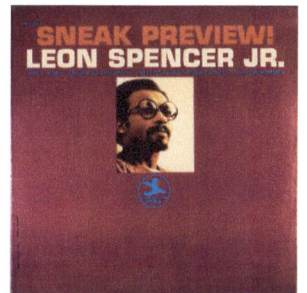

Leon Spencer, Jr.
*Sneak Preview*

Leon Spencer, Jr.
*Louisiana Slim*

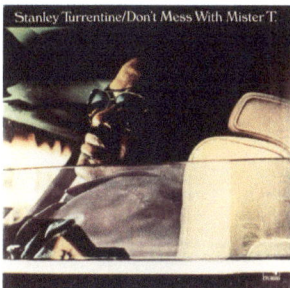

Stanley Turrentine
*Don't Mess with Mister T.*

Grover Washington, Jr.
*Inner City Blues*

Grover Washington, Jr.
*Soul Box*

Reuben Wilson
*Love Bug*

*Hair (The Original Broadway Cast Recording)*

BY KARL HAGSTROM MILLER

Vinyl-heads can smell hard times. Crumbling economies, failed businesses, sky-rocketing rents: each loose coveted vinyl from the crannies and basement storage units they have inhabited for decades. Plant closed? Let me check out the garage sales. Independent record store gone bankrupt? The mother lode. Hands tremble flipping through pristine plastic. The search for oddball records has two cardinal rules: read the transformations of class in the United States, and know that race has every-thing to do with these transformations. Don't be late. Hit the right place at the wrong time. We all know this. Sub-urban thrift stores are typically good for REO and Bob Seger. Gentrifying neighborhoods cause Pete Rodriguez or Doug Carn to float to the surface—for a song. Desperation is the friend of the record collector. Hipness depends on finding a population aggrieved enough to produce good music, suddenly pushed to the point of parting with it.

Case in point: Catskill, New York. The sleepy town of Catskill shares little with its riverfront neighbor, Hudson. The latter's volatile swing from de-industrialized cement town to destination of white flight at least means people are on the streets. The main drag boasts high-end antique shops and the sure sign that the choice vinyl is gone: gour-met coffee. Hudson is currently the sight of a bitter debate about the return of a major cement plant. Many new arriv-als fear that the clouds of white dust will drive away the tourists and settle like a perpetual blanket on their houses and cars. Many old timers fondly remember when cement jobs enabled them to have houses and cars.

Catskill has not had Hudson's one-sided resurgence. Driv-ing up Highway 9w in 1996, one first encountered the dormant cement plant. Main Street boarded up. Unem-ployment rampant. Catskill was a ghost. The only busi-nesses doing any business were on the edge of town: a tattoo parlor and two unassuming junk shops, one selling antique housewares, the other stuffed to the gills with records. It was my favorite kind of shop: volume without design. I couldn't walk down the aisles of the small store. Dusty records and a few odd books were stacked precari-ously everywhere I looked. Slowly making my way through the merchandise, I unpiled half-filled boxes and loose plat-ters to get to what was underneath. I kept asking the aging owner what he wanted for different discs, and after a series of similar responses I caught the pattern. Everything was eight dollars a pop. *Rumors*—dozens, at eight dollars a pop. Rufus—ditto. Twenty thousand or so records all priced the same. A virgin copy of *Gunfighter Ballads* made me hesitate, but, you know, one only needs so many ver-sions of "Cool Water," and I have to *really* like a record to lay down eight bucks.

After about an hour of sifting through shifting piles with-out much to show, I came across a small collection of jazz discs. Several Miles reissues—*At Fillmore* was a bargain at the set price. Underneath were three records in unassum-ing tan covers with black printing. On the back of each, in small type, was the following message:

> This album can be purchased only by mail through the address below and any other form of sale is unauthorized. Send your order and remittance directly to: **Charles Mingus Enterprises, Inc., P.O. Box 2637, Grand Central Station, New York, New York 10017.**

Titles traced life on the road: *Mingus at Monterey; Music Written for Monterey, 1965. Not Heard...Played in Its Entirety at UCLA, Vols. 1 and 2*; and *My Favorite Quin-tet*, recorded live at Minneapolis's Guthrie Theater. Eight bucks apiece brought them home.

The three albums told two stories. One was the hard times that brought them to the proprietor. Junk shops often speak the passion of their owners: vinyl, artwork, military gear. But just as often they collect freight tossed over-board to ease the load. The thousands of albums witnessed people on the move—dislocated and traveling light, leav-ing the accumulated contents of their homes behind.

The second story was just as much about hard times. Charles Mingus Enterprises was the escape plan of a trapped man.

Mingus, who died of Lou Gehrig's disease at the age of fifty-seven in 1979, was one of the great composers of the century. Doubters and revelers can check out grand opuses "Half-Mast Inhibition," "The Shoes of the Fisherman's Wife Are Some Jive Ass Slippers," and "Far Wells, Mill Valley," among countless others. Or dive into the smaller group improvs. "Fables of Faubus" and "Meditations" were spontaneous compositions in his book, starkly different every time they were performed, crackling with new beats, growls—even fresh forms—inspired and executed in the moment. Elements of baroque and stride piano, Dixie-land, Duke, gutbucket, gospel, and atonal wails swirled together in a single song, shattering conceptions of sep-arate genres or styles. Mingus had the unique genius of playing music history and making music history at the same time. And his music swung—OR NOT. It was acces-sible—OR NOT—according to his extraordinary vision.

Yet Mingus the great composer could not pay the bills. He perpetually struggled to make money with his music, even as he saw record executives, concert promoters, and younger, less visionary artists—most of them white—taking cash to the bank. Mingus's life was a roadmap of the intersections of race and economics in the U.S. music industry. The very decision to pick up the bass—an instrument he would quickly push beyond the groundbreaking role pioneered by his hero, Jimmy Blanton—was motivated by race and money. When he met lifelong friend Buddy Collette, young and awkward Mingus was playing cello in his Los Angeles high school orchestra. According to his autobiography, Mingus caught flack from the elder sax player:

> "How'd you like to make bread and wear the sharpest clothes in the latest styles?" Buddy asked… "Go get yourself a bass and we'll put you in our Union swing band…"
>
> "Get a *bass*?"
>
> "That's right. You're black. You'll never make it in classical music no matter how good you are. You want to play, you gotta play a *Negro* instrument. You can't slap a cello, so you gotta learn to *slap that bass*, Charlie!"[1]

Mingus took his friend's advice and got paid. He carted his bass around town, studying with jazz and classical players and practicing even as he rode the trolley back home to Watts. By the early 1940s, he was making dates and a name for himself around the jazz and early R&B scene down Central Avenue, the heart of Black nightlife in Los Angeles. When the wartime recording ban ended, the aspiring musician cast his lot with a series of similarly aspiring local labels. They were looking for jukebox hits. He penned pop-inspired dance tunes such as "The Texas Hop," and "Baby, Take a Chance on Me." Yet he also nodded to the off-kilter harmonies that would dominate his later work with the austere "Weird Nightmare" and brooding arrangements of pop songs "Pennies from Heaven" and "These Foolish Things."[2] Not your average nickel-in-the-slot selections. Mingus wanted to make money with his music, so he dove into the waters open to Black musicians of the era. He played bass. He played jazz. But he insisted on twisting both beyond convention to accommodate the sounds swirling in his head. He was not getting rich.

Mingus picked up the pace. He backed Lionel Hampton. He appreciated the exposure but was frustrated by what he considered his leader's Tomming, not to mention Hampton's insistence on maintaining the publishing rights to tunes Mingus wrote. He left. He needed to get paid. Prestige Records offered to record him for ten bucks and some coke. He left. He toured with Red Norvo and Tal Farlow—an interracial trio that did not make waves due to Mingus's light skin. Then a New York TV producer insisted on using union members. Black musicians had a hard time with the New York union. Norvo, after protesting, replaced him with a white guy. He left, but not with-

out making the most of it. Filing a grievance against Local 802, Mingus won a $500 settlement. After his mother-in-law tossed in another $600, Mingus started his own label with friend Max Roach. They called it Debut Records. It was 1952.[3]

Debut joined a small but vital tradition of Black artists going into business for themselves. Almost as soon as Black musicians caught the notice of existing labels, (signified by Mamie Smith's "Crazy Blues" in 1920), Black entrepreneurs started up their own. They were putting the tenets of Black Nationalism into practice. Harry Pace and W. C. Handy founded Black Swan in 1921. They advertised in the national Black voice, the Chicago *Defender*, telling readers to buy "the Only Genuine Colored Record. Others Are Only Passing for Colored." Black Swan's bread and butter was the blues. Yet Pace and Handy were more interested in showcasing Black classical musicians—artists who were still systematically excluded from major concert venues and recording studios. Black Swan was about access as much as art—money as much as racial uplift. After pulling in over $100,000 in 1921, Black Swan spiraled into debt. They sold their extensive catalog to a white-owned competitor three years later. Other Black-owned labels with names like Sunshine and Meritt came and went as quickly. Later, trumpeter Dizzy Gillespie gave it a shot with his own Dee Gee Records. Again, the label folded in a few years. It was hard to fight the majors.[4]

By the time Mingus and Roach organized Debut Records, the bassist had dived deep into bebop—the frenetic, modernist riff that reclaimed jazz from white swing kings by injecting it with equal parts church, Debussy, and improvisational fire. Bop was suffering the same cultural whiplash that had afflicted swing. One moment, Black innovators such as Gillespie, Charlie Parker, and Kenny Clarke were working under the radar, brewing new sounds in Harlem after-hours clubs. With the nation's ear still tuned to swing, they were not getting paid. The next moment bebop was the rage. It was the soundtrack to white beatnik escapades, fashion shows, and Jiffy-Pop commercials. The innovators were still not getting paid. Debut offered a solution. As Roach recalled, "Nobody was beating down our doors to ask what we were doing. The only way to make records under our own names was to start our own company."[5] Ownership meant reaping the profits from the sale of one's music, not just the one-off payments per selection or the miniscule royalty rates offered by the major labels. It could mean a living. As Mingus quickly discovered, it also meant navigating an apartment overrun by product, licking a lot of mailing labels, and bothering record stores to pay up.

Debut had a nice run. They released several records by the likes of J. J. Johnson, Clifford Brown, and Quincy Jones. Their masterstroke became one of the landmark documents of the bebop era, *Quintet of the Year*, featuring Mingus, Roach, Parker, Gillespie, and pianist Bud Powell. Yet even this victory carried the mark of the trials that had convinced Mingus and Roach to go independent in the first place. Due to contractual obligations, Parker had to use a pseudonym. The local union asserted its control and tried to stop the release of the renegade recordings. And lacking the muscle of the majors, Debut could not get local distributors to pay for the product they had already sold.[6] Debut lasted until 1958, when it collapsed in a heap of uncollected payments and artists' royalty demands.

Meanwhile, Mingus had been gaining a foothold within the larger music industry. His compositional chops were expanding—check out 1956's "Pithecanthropus Erectus" or 1957's "Reincarnation of a Lovebird." He found his ultimate rhythm-section partner in drummer Dannie Richmond. His relentless gigging and recording for various labels, especially a young Atlantic, eventually brought him promising sessions with the behemoth Columbia Records. His initial release for Columbia was a breakout produced by Teo Macero, a Debut alum and future tape-splicer for Miles Davis's electric masterpieces. *Mingus Ah Um* gave the bassist some economic breathing room. With Columbia's marketing power behind it, the record sold much better than his previous releases. It even garnered a hit with album-opener "Better Git It in Your Soul," a rousing gospel-drenched shuffle complete with hand-clapping chorus and, not one, but two, drum breaks. "Boogie Stop Shuffle" hit even harder, recollecting earlier grooves such as "The Texas Hop." Mingus was a name. He started living well. Yet once again, he found his label frustrating his success. Columbia disputed the sales figures for *Mingus Ah Um*, claiming the album sold a paltry 3,000 copies. They suggested the album had been bootlegged.[7] Mingus was enraged.

He took things into his own hands. Charles Mingus Enterprises was going to do it right. He set it up as a mail order business. No majors. No distributors. No retailers. Nobody touching the money passing between the consumer and the composer. He took out ads in music magazines such as *Coda* and the *Village Voice*. They were as much editorial wail as sales pitch. "Among the causes of deprivation in which most musicians live are the avarice and corruption existing in the big business of record companies and their cohorts...**I am doing something more to help free the next, younger generation of jazz music**...LEGAL NOTICE: $500 for evidence which secures conviction of any person for selling these records..."[8] No bootlegs this time. He would not let it happen.

Mingus drew no dividing line between American racism and the economic exploitation he found in the music industry. The liner notes to Charles Mingus Enterprises' second release, *Town Hall Concert*, launched a thinly veiled attack on Columbia's John Hammond.

This Negro-discovering, self-endowed enemy not only to the black man, do I charge him and his efforts to further keep righteousness from my black donkey brothers, I charge this ham-am the enemy of all freedom, green, red, black, yellow, English, French: 'There ain't no white man except in America...' Why he wouldn't give a starving puppy a bone, let alone pay his taxes from the money he earned on this axis, as Birds blow their axes—can't get fair money or enough to-lax...John Doe relax? Schitt old John, Hamhead, is the ax and the tax.

Charles Mingus Enterprises would be different, he insisted.

After we pay the musicians, the band, as a cooperative group, will receive a minimum of 7–10%. We'll be the first company to do this and we'll find out why so many people can't sell our record under the table like John Hamhead said must happen...This will be the first American company to make a step to give justice to all employed. When we succeed, we will also practice fair employment—and not just blacks—we will employ an equal amount of human labor outside of the recorded music world—like secretaries, business executives—compared to the mathematician's statistics of integrated peoples in the NYC area, or any other city we expand to.

Referring to his band and concert organizer Mrs. Dupree White of the NAACP, he concluded, "With disgust for the American recording industry, I give you, the public, this day seven people set to free themselves in music."[9] It was a declaration of independence.

Charles Mingus Enterprises' first release was *Mingus at Monterey*, a double disc stuffed into a single sleeve chronicling his triumphant debut at the 1964 Monterey Jazz Festival. The album featured three sweeping works. A touching Ellington medley concluded with Mingus explaining, "I imagine I should say 'I love you madly' at this point, because if there is a recording the money will all go to Duke Ellington, which is about due him. I've stolen it." If there was any doubt, money was on his mind. Yet he was thinking music as well. "Orange Was the Color of Her Dress, Then Blue Silk" was followed by a big band arrangement of "Meditations on Integration." A bowed bass line gave way to rolling woodwinds. Mingus slowly built a soundtrack to an imagined epic by stacking melodies one upon another. Then he abruptly jumped into a vicious swinging ensemble workout under a crying sax solo. Mingus pushed the band through a dozen dazzling sections before breaking down into a smoldering conversation between his bass and Jaki Byard's piano. "Meditations" was an encyclopedia. Music history—jazz, classical, folk, free-form—integrated into one seamless score. The crowd went nuts.

Upon its release, orders rolled in for *Mingus at Monterey*. Even Mingus was surprised by the results. Small checks started stacking up in his apartment. He quickly prepared three more releases. *Town Hall Concert* and *My Favorite Quintet* featured his small ensembles. *Monterey* at times had the tension of a band about to collapse under its own weight. *Town Hall* and *Favorite Quintet* were spry, agile, able to soar. Without the added horns, the music opened up, and Dannie Richmond's astounding drumming came to the fore.

Richmond played with Mingus for twenty-two years. Mingus molded the former sax player into his image of what a drummer should be: elastic, organic, conversational. Together, they defined the Mingus rhythmic ideal and created some of the most breathing, funky grooves around. Richmond could play orchestrally behind the composer's written sections, emphasizing the form and holding together the often-disparate strands of melody. Yet it was under extended solos that the rhythm section really went to work. Check out "Praying with Eric" on *Town Hall*. They mixed it up constantly. Second line. Swing. Stop time. Double time. Latin. Polka. Some grooves lasted no more than a measure or two. Mingus and Richmond created a fluid yet shifting foundation for the horns to do their work—suggesting many later funk and hip-hop experiments with a flowing progression of changing beats. The two locked into a rhythmic embrace.

The fourth release by Charles Mingus Enterprises was another concert of ambitious large ensemble pieces. Following his 1964 success at Monterey, Mingus had big plans for the 1965 festival. He prepared works that would challenge "Meditations" in scope and theatricality. They had names like "Once Upon a Time There Was a Holding Corporation Called Old America," "They Trespass the Land of the Sacred Sioux," and "Don't Be Afraid, the Clown's Afraid Too." Money got in the way. When several boxes of *Mingus at Monterey* failed to arrive at the festival, Mingus saw sure sales dissolve into missed opportunity. He blamed the festival promoter for the snafu and walked off stage in disgust after a twenty-minute set.[10] He had trouble building momentum.

A week later he presented the music at UCLA. He released the concert on a double disc titled *Music Written for Monterey, 1965. Not Heard…Played in Its Entirety, at UCLA. Vols. 1 and 2.* "Meditations on Inner Peace" opened the show with a near twenty-minute drummerless dirge. It was not typical Mingus. After two false starts on "Holding Corporation," Mingus sent the extra horns backstage to practice before launching into a quartet tribute titled "Ode to Bird and Diz." The return of the chastised members brought a whirlwind of orchestral jazz, sounding like a circus band playing ragtime in a Weimar cabaret. It was aching and ambitious, if under-rehearsed. The show ended with "Don't Let It Happen Here," a musical adaptation of a poem by German anti-fascist Pastor Niemöller. In 1966, Mingus released 200 copies of the concert, complete with liner notes linking Nazi scientific experiments to police brutality and the Watts rebellion that had occurred just before his UCLA gig.

That was it for Charles Mingus Enterprises. Four albums in two years. His life was falling apart. Mail requests for albums went unanswered. The Better Business Bureau logged complaints. He was evicted from his New York loft.

**Newswe**

**Herald Tribun**

By Ralph J. Gle
*A Special Correspo*
MONTEREY, C

It took the Monter
Festival six years
around to inviting
composer and instrum
Charles Mingus to
but when it finally h
the result was worth
for.

Mingus, in a nerve-
Sunday afternoon p
erased the memory
other bass player in
his virtuoso playir
added a new dimer
Monterey's Reputat
providing musical s

Mingus appeared v
small group, includir
ist Jackie Byard a
saxophonist Charles
son, in a medley of
compositions and
Mingus' own numbera
forceful and strongly
ing music.

Then Mingus with
reappear a few mome
with an augmented c
of 11 pieces and to
composition, "Med
which was so strikir
impact that he rec
standing ovation at
clusion, and musicia
stage cheered him.

"Meditations" was
tation of a longer w
was replete with bo
plucked passages by
poser, a poignant f
by Buddy Collette an
series of rising dis
that created an extr
musical tension.
years Monterey has
avant-garde jazz, bu
fort by Mingus s
them all. Despite th
spontaneity (nurture
composer's own info
and dances of joy o
it was the result of
of intensive rehears
worked.

Mingus' triumph
first half of the Su
ernoon program, s
5,000 people sat in
ing Monterey sunsh
horse show arena
Monterey County fa

Wife Are Some Jive Ass Slippers." *Let My Children Hear Music* was something of a retrospective touching on different aspects of his art: ballet scores, Latin tinges, blues. They even resurrected "The Chill of Death," a word jazz piece Mingus penned back when he was recording juke box numbers for independents in Los Angeles. The album covered it all, and recorded it beautifully. He was an elder statesman. He began to make money again, even as much of the earnings from record sales were going straight to Columbia.

Charles Mingus Enterprises became a footnote to his long career, an ambitious—some believed foolhardy—attempt to change the world. Mingus tried to reinvent the way music and money were made. He was only half successful. Charles Mingus Enterprises was a financial failure.

Record collectors love footnotes to history. Great artist plus failed plans equals expensive gems. The three albums I picked up in Catskill glistened. The discs had the luminous sheen of virgin vinyl. The covers were intact. They were well protected for several decades before they were dumped on the heap at the Catskill junk shop. They had the added value of being extremely rare, especially *Not Heard*. Think about it. Original recordings of major works by one of the nation's great Black jazz men. Political music from the era of Black Power. No distribution. Only a handful pressed before the masters were lost. The equation ends with a price guide listing for one thousand dollars. Dealers salivate at the sight of this stuff. Their blank expressions belie the questions rumbling through their heads. "Where in the world did he find them?" "Why wasn't I there?" "How much do I offer to make them mine?" The traffic in rare vinyl, particularly in Black musicians only belatedly celebrated by white enthusiasts, often makes far more money off the music than did the original artists. Their fly-by-night venture, their lack of distribution, their inability to get paid are all cash in the bank to the savvy collector. Desperation is the friend of the record hound.

I was not above financial considerations myself. I could woe afford to keep precious gems on my shelf. I dubbed the discs before selling them to a New York dealer and buying a laptop. ●

Film crews caught him weeping as city workers loaded his belongings into a dump truck.[11] In desperation, Mingus dumped his dream of autonomy within the music industry and signed a distribution agreement with his friends at Fantasy Records. The reissue of *Mingus at Monterey* was accompanied by a heartfelt plea from Mingus for personal contributions. The UCLA tapes languished in the storage facilities at Columbia before they were tossed out during a general housecleaning. Mingus slipped from view, tired, broke, and confused.

The '70s would find him resurfacing. The publication of his sensationalist autobiography in 1971 brought press clippings. He got back in the graces of Columbia. Teo Macero came on board for an album of large-scale works. They recorded selections from the UCLA concert. "Don't Be Afraid" burned far hotter than the original. "Holding Corporation" was redubbed "The Shoes of the Fisherman's

*When* Karl Hagstrom Miller *is not sifting through stacks of old vinyl or spinning his pristine copy of* Pink Panther Punk*, he is a doctoral student at New York University. His current project is a book titled* Folklore, Phonographs, and the Segregation of Southern Music. *He lives and plays music in Austin, Texas.*

Notes:

1. Charles Mingus, *Beneath the Underdog* (New York: Penguin, 1971), p. 52.

2. Mingus's independent label sides have been reissued on *Charles 'Baron' Mingus: West Coast 1945–1949* (Uptown UPCD 27.48, 2000).

3. Gene Santro, *Myself When I Am Real: The Life and Music of Charles Mingus* (Oxford: Oxford University Press, 2000), pp. 74–75, 90–102.

4. Ted Vincent, *Keep Cool: The Black Activists who Built the Jazz Age* (London: Pluto Press, 1995), pp. 92–105; William Barlow, *Looking Up at Down: The Emergence of Blues Culture* (Philadelphia: Temple University Press, 1989), p. 128.

5. *Ibid.*, p. 97.

6. *Ibid.*, pp. 102–105.

7. *Ibid.*, p. 240.

8. *Coda* (April-May 1965); quoted in Brian Priestley, *Mingus: A Critical Biography* (New York: Da Capo Press, 1982), p. 164.

9. Liner notes to Charles Mingus, *Town Hall Concert*, 1964 (Charles Mingus Enterprises JWS 005, 1966); reissued as Fantasy OJC-042).

10. Priestley, *Mingus*, pp. 166–167.

11. The eviction is captured in Tom Reichman's documentary, *Mingus* (1968).

# CHARLIE MINGUS FINGERS THE RECORD HI-JACKERS

# BUILDING BLOCKS

by andrew mason

It was 1987, and I was making my regular pilgrimage to Music Factory in Times Square, searching for goodies of the audible kind. Passing the Buddha-like figure of Stanley Platzer, the store manager who seemed permanently ensconced behind a small counter near the front of the store, I eagerly flipped through the latest releases on labels like Cold Chillin', Prism, Fresh, and First Priority.

On the wall there were a few mysterious records that caught my eye. Looking over the titles, I saw things like "Apache," "Big Beat," "Honky Tonk Woman," but no artists were listed. Were these some Pickwick-style knock-offs by a no-name cover band? Why were songs by the Rolling Stones and Billy Squier, two bands that personified mainstream rock-n-roll, loitering in the prime real estate of wall space reserved for the hottest slices of the underground music then known as "new school rap"? I didn't know, and didn't give it much thought, quickly snatching up the "Pickin' Boogers" and "Juice Crew Dis" singles.

Flashback to a few years before. Late at night, high up on the radio dial, I would occasionally hear weird collages of music that seeped into my subconscious and laid the foundation that would eventually explain this phenomena to me. Cheech and Chong talkin' some bullshit, suddenly a heavy beat pounded through (that made even a playin'-the-wall herb like me want to shake my pants), repeating and stuttering back on itself, then—wait, what's that weird electronic outer space-sounding noise…into something that sounds like "White Lines," but I know that's not Melle Mel. I rummaged through a shoebox to find a tape I could record over.

Rap music had been sort of a novelty for me; I was not a b-boy from the Bronx, simply a kid into music. The popular rap hits of the early '80s were records I bought, but they didn't hold any particular prominence over the rest of the pop music of the day. But by the mid-'80s, things had changed. I had always been an avid taper of radio shows, and my ear steadily gravitated towards the sounds I was hearing. When I discovered stores like Music Factory, I made them my mecca, quickly becoming a fanatic of what were clearly the freshest sounds out there.

As sampling became more prevalent, I started to hear elements in the new jams that I recognized. I couldn't quite place most of them, but they were familiar as a Beatles melody. A friend hipped me to the fact that a funky cowbell riff I loved so much was in fact from a song called "Mardi Gras." I started examining those cheap-looking records that had SUPER DISCO BRAKES written in big block type across the front, and soon enough came across one with a song that fit the description. I placed the record with the off-center orange and black label on the turntable, dropped the needle on the first track, and, with that sensation that only vinyl can give, waited for the tune to kick in. Huh? The needle must've jumped, because there was my cowbell jam, but it wasn't playing right. Examining the record, I couldn't see anything wrong. I later found that every single pressing of that record had that skip in it (and still does; check out *Super Disco Brakes Vol. 1*). Thank you, Paul Winley.

In spite of this technical difficulty, a flame had been sparked which only gained in intensity. I quickly graduated to the superior pressings of Street Beat Records' *Ultimate Breaks & Beats* series, then in its prime—already to fourteen volumes or so by the time I got to them. *UBB #9* was my toe in the water, and I was immediately hooked. This article is a study, an attempt to get at why tunes on these records have such resonance, but above all a tribute to an essential ingredient of hip-hop.

There is a logical starting point when attempting to understand this culture that has grown from the roots of hip-hop and flowered into what we call beatdigging. When a fledgling beat-maker is getting started there is essential 101 knowledge. You crawl before you walk, and when it comes to this game, crawling means learning the foundation: the beats and breaks that gave birth to hip-hop. These tunes are our music theory and history, the rules you need to know before you can break them.

If all this seems abstract and removed from where we're at these days, let me take you back. A party, just getting bubbling. The room is not too big, not too small. A few groups of ladies, some fellas maintaining neutral ground. The DJ has a stack of 45s in front of him and has begun cueing up the next. The groove sends a wave of bass up from your feet, meeting the highs and mids in your chest and causing an involuntary ripple of your torso. The fellas nod. The ladies swing heads appreciatively. Alright. Suddenly a grin breaks out on one of your boys. He has heard the intro for the next song being brought in. BAM! The DJ brings the fader over and the rest of the room shares

the joy as energy starts building up in the rapidly filling room. It doesn't stop there, feet begin shuffling as drums you have heard since childhood get worked out, snapping and splintering as the DJ gets busy with two copies of the same joint. The next jam comes in and by now somebody is going for theirs, body working in time to a groove as sweet and familiar as the fragrance of spring. The next record hits the spot like a perfect pick-and-roll, and you know you're in the right place. The room is full and the party is live, and it's just begun.

Beautiful, right? Don't think this is some late '70s flashback, though. This scene took place less than a month ago, late 2001, as I was finishing up this article. The DJ was Spinna, the location was a basement club in Manhattan, and nearly all the joints that got everyone so open can be found in one place: the *UBB* series.

*Ultimate Breaks & Beats* is essentially a catalog of rhythm. The 150-plus songs it compiles over its twenty-five volumes demonstrate an impressive array of 4/4 drum patterns and variations that form a textbook for any rhythmatist looking to generate motion, whether your kit is an Akai, Technics, or Ludwig.

To take it further, a case can be made that the breaks featured on Street Beat's *Ultimate Breaks & Beats* series form the basis for modern popular rhythm. This thesis does not seem so far-fetched when you trace the roots of contemporary electronic and dance styles and their indebtedness to rap music and its production techniques. It's a chronology that leads from community center parties in Harlem and the Bronx to the rise of sampling in the mid-'80s and onward to the creations of the dance music innovators who were inspired by the rhythm patterns of rap music.

Avant-garde experimentalists like Karlheinz Stockhausen, John Cage, and Steve Reich worked with primal "samples" (tape loops) in the '50s and '60s, and music professionals in the '70s used expensive machines like the Fairlight and the Mellotron to imitate various live instruments. It wasn't until the mid-'80s, however, that digital sampling equipment began to come within the reach of non-professional musicians.

As sampling became an option for more folks involved in making music, it was a natural step to take the funkiest pieces of party classics and loop them, thereby imitating

the feel of a DJ running a break with two copies of the same record. Grandmaster Flash explains the concept: "My main objective was to take small parts of records…maybe forty seconds, keeping it going for about five minutes."[1] In fact, this strategy was employed well before samplers came into use. Keith LeBlanc, drummer on many of the early Sugar Hill records, related this story: "Sylvia [Robinson, Sugar Hill Records president] would be at Harlem World or Disco Fever, and she'd watch who was mixing what four bars off of what record. She'd get that record, and then she'd play us those four bars and have us go in and cut it better."[2]

In 1985, E-mu introduced the SP12 sampling drum machine, and soon after that sampling started to pop up in rap music. Rick Rubin redid LL Cool J's "Rock the Bells" using a large chunk of Trouble Funk as its rhythmic bed (the original version of "Bells" was all drum machine), while Marley Marl hooked Biz Markie up with "The Biz Dance" (graced by drum hits chopped from Rufus Thomas's "Do the Funky Penguin") and "Make the Music with Your Mouth Biz" (Isaac Hayes, in fact, making much of the music with his piano via a nice sample). Ced Gee handled production for Ultramagnetic MC's and Boogie Down Productions, creating the amazing "Ego Trippin'" with little more than an SP12 and a loungey-sounding 7-inch with a dope drum break. The usage of James Brown on BDP's "South Bronx" kicked off a long (unrequited) love affair between samplists and the Godfather of Soul (Double Dee & Steinski had used liberal chunks of Soul Brother #1 as early as 1984 on their landmark remix of "Play that Beat Mr. DJ" by G.L.O.B.E. & Whiz Kid).

So where did folks go for their source material, the sure shot beats that would resonate with such power in their listeners? Some had access to record collections of their parents and the creativity to use them, but for many, the most convenient way to obtain these essential beats was through break compilations.

Street Beat Records, the company that distributed *UBB*, was incorporated in 1986 by a car service driver and part-time DJ named Lenny Roberts, aka Breakbeat Lenny. It was not the first or only label reissuing what was called B-Beat (Break Beat) music. There were plenty of one-off "Disco Mixer" 12-inches that edited up-tempo disco breakdowns together for the club jocks, and 12-inch bootleg reedits of anthems like "Scratchin'" (extended past eight minutes) and "Apache" that had been around since the late '70s. Paul Winley's infamous *Super Disco Brakes* series was in lo-fi effect straight out of 125th Street, and the equally infamous but more mysterious *Octopus* (as the no-named series is commonly referred to) records were coming out of Florida by way of the Bronx. Much more obscure, these direct predecessors of the *UBB* series date to 1980 and are the Pithecanthropus erectus to *UBB*'s Homo sapiens. The *Octopus* track listing is duplicated almost exactly on the first ten *Ultimate Breaks* records, raising questions about the relationship between the two.

In an article published in 1988, Lenny Roberts claimed that the *Octopus* records were put out by "some guy in the Bronx," and stressed that he (in contrast) "wrote away for all the licensing" on his comps. So where did the *Octopus* originate? I talked to a longtime employee of NYC's Downstairs Records who told me about a series of doo-wop bootlegs making the rounds in the mid- to late '70s, allegedly mafia-sponsored. The compiler, apparently also an aspiring cartoonist, adorned these bootlegs with various anthropomorphic animal characters. Thus the *Octopus*—with its image cheerfully cueing up a couple of records under the words "Break Beats," a phone to one ear and headphones to the other—was likely just an attempt to diversify the market. This theory is supported by the location of the manufacturer of the *Octopus* boots: Hollywood, Florida, a well-known wiseguy ward.

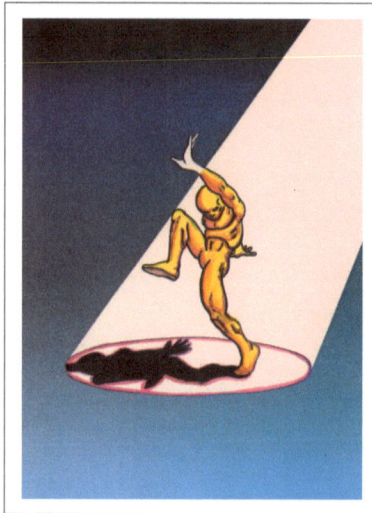

*Octopus #7* and *#8* became the *UBB* "mystery" LPs (SBR-507 and SBR-508), probably more available in *Octopus* form than on the rapidly discontinued Street Beat pressings of these two volumes (rumor has it that John Davis threatened lawsuits over the inclusion of his "I Can't Stop" on SBR-507 and that the master for SBR-508 was lost). Beyond these two and a song that appeared on some pressings of *Octopus #4* called "Get Up" (Pookie Blow rhyming over the "Dance to the Drummer's Beat" break), the *Octopus* survives to this day in the guise of *UBB*.

What sets Street Beat's *Ultimate Breaks* apart from all its competitors is its sheer longevity, its superior sound quality, and most of all, being in the right place at the right time.

The series is fascinating on several levels. For one, the fusion of styles it contains demands the listener disregard notions of genre. This is a mind-set that is perhaps not as revolutionary as it once was, but at the time it was like lightning bottled, a roots tonic straight out of the witch doctor's apothecary. After all, playlists of these records were copped from party favorites spun by Bambaataa,

Herc, even David Mancuso (by way of GM Flash). *UBB* was the series that really broke the original "wall of silence" surrounding breakbeat music and set a precedent in break compilations.

I spoke to David Mancuso about how he feels seeing records he introduced at his legendary Loft parties end up on break records. Although his attitude towards unauthorized copies of tunes isn't positive ("I don't like bootlegs!"), Mancuso has always been about spreading the love when it comes to hot tracks. He was one of the founders of the first record pool (the New York Record Pool, founded in 1974), a system devised to keep influential DJs stocked with the latest, greatest tunes. In exchange for new releases, members of the pool were required to rate records according to their personal reaction and to the floor reaction when it was played. One of the members of the record pool was Joseph Saddler, aka Grandmaster Flash. Afrika Bambaata was also in attendance at Loft parties, where records like "Woman" by Barrabas (originally picked up by Mancuso at a flea market in Amsterdam) and Lonnie Liston Smith's "Expansions" were in heavy rotation. These tunes quickly made their way uptown and from there eventually onto the *UBB* comps.

Both the *Octopus* and the Street Beat records share the sometimes useful, sometimes infuriating trait of looping breaks within certain songs. The idea was to make short breaks easier to catch, but in some cases this resulted in uncomfortably stiff edits such as on Lyn Collins's "Think" or Dyke & the Blazers' "Let a Woman Be a Woman, Let a Man Be a Man." Louis Flores, credited with editing the tracks, used another interesting technique that occurs a couple times in the series: the pitch change. "UFO" by ESG was originally issued by 99 Records on a 45 rpm 12-inch. The grinding, heavy groove heard on *UBB #9* is the result of hearing this record at the lower, wrong, turntable tempo setting (play your break record at 45 to hear it as it was originally recorded). Dexter Wansel's stately "Theme From the Planets" gets flipped by reversing this method, sending it into warp drive on 45. Even weirder is the edit on the Winstons' "Amen Brother." It sounds like Flores pitched down this crazy up-tempo drum break by simply tapping the 33/45 buttons once at the beginning of the break, then again at the end to bring the song back to its intended pitch.

Flores also tacked vocal phrases onto various cuts, these fall into the category of DJ tools. Most notable is "(Runaway) Wouldn't Change a Thing," an excerpt from a Thomas "Coke" Escovedo LP. On the original album, the last vocal shout of "Runaway" precedes the percussion intro to "Wouldn't Change a Thing" by several seconds—typical track spacing on an album. On *UBB #13* the gap is removed, making it easier for DJs to imitate the routine Flash used when he would scratch the vocal shout over the next tune's breakbeat intro.

The series combined the obvious with the unheard-of. It doesn't take long to find such unlikely comrades as Rufus Thomas and Gary Numan (#22) or the Rolling Stones rubbing shoulders with an obscure Italian disco band (#2). Long before folks like Gilles Peterson or Keb Darge were compiling impossibly rare 7-inches for mass consumption, Street Beat ensured that thousands of DJs and aficionados had copies of obscure cuts like "Impeach the President" by the enigmatic Honey Drippers or Please's Philipino funk version of "Sing a Simple Song."

Neither *Octopus* nor *UBB* listed artists for any of their songs, however. As Lenny Roberts said, the *UBB* series does include publishing information, but that's it. Whether the decision to not include artists' names was a result of publishing rights (or lack of them) or a code of honor is debatable. The legendary level of secrecy surrounding break records was tight, and, to this day, a big part of the competition that goes on among DJs is finding a record that your brethren are not up on. In the late '70s, when the Zulu Nation and the Herculords sound systems were battling, it was all about volume and coming up with that mystery joint that caught you out thereand made you rush the decks to catch a glimpse of the label. First-wave innovators such as Kool Herc, Bam, Jazzy Jay, and Flash made a science out of unearthing these obscure rhythmic riffs that would not only move the crowd but confound their rivals as well. Many felt that it was out of bounds for anyone to be revealing ingredients.

> *"It took a little bit of that mystery out of it, 'cause it was hard to find these records. You didn't find them every day of the week. When Lenny made them available, it was like, anybody can have them now."*
> —Jazzy Jay[3]

But for a new generation of fans who never saw Bam rock the parks in the Bronx, these comps were gold. As Kenny "Dope" Gonzalez, told me, "I'm down with them, 'cause they taught a lot of us about breaks. They were key in a lot of people's collections, even though people knock them." Renowned breakbeat aficionado DJ Spinna related, "I picked up my first *Ultimate Breaks* in '85. There used to be a store on 42nd Street where cats went to get all the bootleg breakbeat 12-inches like 'Impeach the President' and 'Funky President,' which are even harder to get than the *Octopus* joints." For many contemporary masters, *UBB* was school—or, as Q-Bert put it in his barnstorming tour through the Street Beat series, preschool (DJ Q-Bert, *Demolition Pumpkin Squeeze – A Pre School Break Mix*).

Of course, fame will bring its share of biters. From the disco/electro-oriented Street Beat bootlegs with pre-*UBB* catalog numbers SBR-498, SBR-499, and SBR-500 (the actual Street Beat series started at SBR-501) to bootleg versions of the discontinued #7, there have been countless coattail-riding copycat compilations. The popular *Diggin'* series, now in double digits, started as a blatant *UBB* spin-off, shamelessly titling the inaugural LP *Ultimate Breaks & Beats #26*. Before you could say, "Yo, you could catch a smack for that," this blasphemy was corrected; on subsequent pressings, the brash upstart reverted to its proper moniker, *Diggin' (Vol. 1)*.

These days the shelves of record stores are littered with similar *spot-the-sample*-type break compilations and reissues seemingly intent on turning over every last funky rock. Looking at the role these comps play now, it may be hard to understand or remember the weight *UBB* held during its prime. The pinnacle of *UBB*'s influence was probably in 1987–88, when it was not uncommon for hip-hop tracks and even LPs to be based almost wholly on tracks contained in the latest *UBB*. Many classic singles released in that time, like "My Philosophy" (BDP), "It's My Thing" (EPMD), "I Know You Got Soul" (Eric B. & Rakim) and "It Takes Two" (Rob Base & DJ E-Z Rock), fit this description.

As the '80s came to a close, breakbeat culture had moved far from its roots. Innovative beatmakers began disdaining the now well-known breaks on *UBB* and the series lost steam. Cuts began to be included *because* they had been sampled, rather than for their established fame with the b-boys (a group rapidly being overwhelmed in number by "rap" fans who often had little connection to the culture that gave birth to the music). All the People's "Cramp Your Style," the basis for BDP's "Still #1," found its way onto #21 a year or so after BDP used it. AJ Woodson, better known as AJ Rok of JVC Force, told me, "I sampled Freda Payne's "Easiest Way to Fall" [the B-side of "Band of Gold"] off both her 45 and her album. It was added to the breakbeat album some two or three years after we used it because we used it [on 'Strong Island']." The track appeared on #23, issued towards the end of 1989.

Street Beat would only release two more LPs in the series, #24 and the final twentieth "Silver Anniversary" edition appearing in 1991. Over ten years have passed, but, to this day, the records are still available, still essential, still the king. ●

*When he's not playing scrabble over cocktails with Walt "Clyde" Frazier, ANDREW MASON can be found finger-painting with his daughter in their Brooklyn bungalow. As DJ MONK ONE, he spins Saturdays on Jay Smooth's "Underground Railroad Show" on WBAI 99.5 FM, NYC.*

Notes:

1. David Toop, *Rap Attack* (London: Pluto Press, 1984), p.63.

2. *Village Voice* (Jan. 19, 1988).

3. *Ibid.*

# Ultimate Breaks & Beats Complete Discography

| SONG | ARTIST | YEAR | LABEL | AS LISTED ON *UBB*/NOTES |
|------|--------|------|-------|--------------------------|
| **SBR-501 (1986)** | | | | |
| * Mary, Mary | The Monkees | 1967 | Colgems/RCA | |
| * Black Grass | Wilbur "Bad" Bascomb | 1972 | Paramount | |
| * Amen, Brother | The Winstons | 1969 | Metromedia | Opening drum break is pitched down (switches from 45 to 33 rpm); the rest of the song is at normal pitch. |
| * Daisy Lady | 7th Wonder | 1979 | Parachute | |
| * Indiscreet | D.C. LaRue | 1976 | Pyramid | Only 4:53 of the 12-inch version are used. |
| * Do the Funky Penguin | Rufus Thomas | 1972 | Stax | |
| **SBR-502 (1986)** | | | | |
| * Get Me Back on Time, Engine No. 9 | Wilson Pickett | 1970 | Atlantic | Listed as "Get Me Back on Time." |
| * Catch a Groove | Juice | 1976 | Greedy | 12-inch version |
| * Honky Tonk Women | The Rolling Stones | 1967 | London | |
| You'll Like It Too | Funkadelic | 1981 | LAX | |
| The Boogie Back | Roy Ayers Ubiquity | 1974 | Polydor | |
| * Chella Llá | Orchestra Internazionale | 1974 | Fiesta | Commonly referred to as "Disco Italiano," the title of the Orchestra Internazionale LP. |
| **SBR-503 (1986)** | | | | |
| Got to Be Real | Cheryl Lynn | 1978 | Columbia | |
| Apache | Incredible Bongo Band | 1973 | MGM/Pride | |
| Dance to the Drummer's Beat | Herman Kelly & Life | 1978 | Electric Cat | |
| * Bongo Rock | Incredible Bongo Band | 1973 | MGM/Pride | |
| Give It to You | UPP | 1975 | Epic | |
| * Pussy Footer | Jackie Robinson | 1977 | Direction | |
| **SBR-504 (1986)** | | | | |
| * Different Strokes | Syl Johnson | 1967 | Twinight | |
| * I Know You Got Soul | Bobby Byrd | 1971 | King | |
| * I Think I'd Do It | Z.Z. Hill | 1972 | Mankind | |
| Sing Sing | Gaz | 1978 | Salsoul | |
| Breakthrough | Isaac Hayes | 1974 | Enterprise | |
| Funky Music Is the Thing, Pt. 2 | Dynamic Corvettes | 1975 | Abet | Part 2 of the 45 version. |
| **SBR-505 (1986)** | | | | |
| * Shifting Gears | Johnny Hammond | 1975 | Milestone | |
| * Hit or Miss | Bo Diddley | 1974 | Chess | Listed as "Hit and Miss." |
| Soul, Soul, Soul | The Wild Magnolias | 1974 | Polydor | |
| * Synthetic Substitution | Melvin Bliss | 1973 | Sunburst | Listed as "Substitution." |
| Get Up and Dance | Freedom | 1979 | Malaco | 12-inch version |
| Heaven and Hell | 20th Century Steel Band | 1975 | Island | |
| * Shack Up (part II) | Banbarra | 1975 | United Artists | "Listed as "Shack Up." |
| **SBR-506 (1986)** | | | | |
| * Sing a Simple Song | Please | 1975 | Philips | |
| * Cold Sweat | James Brown | 1967 | King | |
| * Theme from 2001 | Cecil Holmes Soulful Sounds | 1973 | Buddha | Listed as "Black Motion Picture Experience," actually the title of the Cecil Holmes Soulful Sounds LP. |
| * Son of Scorpio | Dennis Coffey | 1973 | Sussex | |
| * Scratchin' | Magic Disco Machine | 1975 | Motown | |
| Down on the Avenue | Fat Larry's Band | 1976 | WMOT | |
| I Like Funky Music | Uncle Louie | 1979 | Marlin | 12-inch version |
| **SBR-507 (1986)** | | | | |
| Give It Up or Turnit a Loose | James Brown | 1969 | King | The "live" version from the *Sex Machine* LP. |
| Street-Talk (Madam Rapper) Instrumental | The Funky Constellation | 1979 | Frozen Butterfly | |
| Let's Dance | Pleasure | 1976 | Fantasy | |
| I Can't Stop | John Davis | 1976 | Sam | 12-inch version |
| * Planetary Citizen | Mahavishnu Orchestra/John McLaughlin | 1976 | Milestone | |
| Good Ole Music | Funkadelic | 1970 | Invictus | |
| You Are What You Are | William Ray | 1977 | Magic Touch | |
| **SBR-508 (1986)** | | | | |
| The Mexican | Babe Ruth | 1973 | Harvest | Re-released on SBR-513 |
| Frisco Disco | Eastside Connection | 1978 | Rampart | Re-released on SBR-513 |
| Flip | Jesse Green | 1977 | Epic | 12-inch version |
| Bring It Here | Wild Sugar | 1980 | TSOB | Re-released on SBR-519 |
| Hand Clapping Song | The Meters | 1970 | Josie | Re-released on SBR-513 |
| Midnight Theme | Manzel | 1979 | Fraternity | |
| Two Pigs and a Hog | Cooley High Soundtrack | 1975 | Motown | |
| It's My Thing | Marva Whitney | 1969 | King | Re-released on SBR-518 |
| **SBR-509 (1986)** | | | | |
| Easter Parade | Ingrid | 1982 | | |
| * UFO | ESG | 1981 | 99 | Originally pressed on a 45 rpm ep, this version is pitched down (to 33 rpm). |
| Big Beat | Billy Squier | 1980 | Capitol | |
| Cavern | Liquid Liquid | 1983 | 99 | |
| * Long Red | Mountain | 1972 | Windfall | From the Mountain *Live* LP; the studio version has no drum break. |

* Song has been edited/manipulated

Seven Minutes of Funk...........Tyrone Thomas & the Whole Darn Family ..1976 ... Amherst ................The Amherst label version was used; there is different mix of the same song on Soul International Records.

**SBR-510 (1986)**
Funky President..........James Brown ...........1974 ... Polydor
* Theme from the Planets ...........Dexter Wansel ............1976 ... Philadelphia Int'l.....Track has been pitched up (from 33 to 45 rpm).
Theme from S.W.A.T ...........Rhythm Heritage ..........1978 ... ABC
* It's Great To Be Here ..........The Jackson Five ...........1971 ... Motown
Ain't We Funkin' Now ..........The Brothers Johnson .........1978 ... A & M ...............12-inch version
* Shangri La..........La Pregunta ..........1978 ... GNP Crescendo ......12-inch 33 rpm version (12-inch 45 rpm version has a saxophone solo over the drum break).
* Last Night Changed It All ..........Esther Williams .........1976 ... Friends & Co.........12-inch version; 7-inch version is identical but does not have the telephone ring on the intro.

**SBR-511 (1986)**
* Impeach the President ..........Honey Drippers ...........1973 ... Alaga
* God Make Me Funky ..........Headhunters ...........1975 ... Arista ...............Listed as "God Make Me Funny," uses 3:00 of the LP version.
Gotta Get Out of Here ...........Lucy Hawkins ...........1978 ... SAM
* Action ..........Orange Krush ..........1982 ... Mercury
Kool Is Back ..........Funk Inc. ...........1971 ... Prestige
* Love's Theme ..........Fausto Papetti ...........1975 ... Durium

**SBR-512 (1986)**
* Granny's Funky Rolls Royce ...........Junie ...........1975 ... Westbound ............Uses only the vocal intro from the 3:41 original.
* Funky Drummer ..........James Brown ...........1970 ... Polydor
The Champ...........Mohawks...........1968 ... Pama
* Walk This Way ...........Aerosmith...........1975 ... Columbia
Johnny the Fox...........Thin Lizzy...........1978 ... Vertigo
Ashley's Roachclip ...........Soul Searchers ...........1974 ... Sussex
* Gangster Boogie ...........Chicago Gangsters ...........1975 ... Gold Mind
Groove to Get Down ...........T-Connection ...........1977 ... TK

**SBR-513 (1987)**
The Mexican...........Babe Ruth ...........1973 ... Harvest
* Keep Your Distance ...........Babe Ruth ...........1976 ... Capitol
* I Wouldn't Change a Thing ...........Coke Escovedo ...........1976 ... Mercury...........Listed as "(Runaway) Wouldn't Change a Thing)," the final seconds of Escovedo's "Runaway" has been tacked on as the intro.
Frisco Disco ...........Eastside Connection ...........1978 ... Rampart
Phenomena Theme ...........In Search Of Orchestra ...........1977 ... AVI
Hand Clapping Song ...........The Meters ...........1970 ... Josie

**SBR-514 (1987)**
* Sister Sanctified ...........Stanley Turrentine ...........1972 ... CTI
Willie Chase ...........J.J. Johnson ...........1974 ... MCA
Uphill Peace of Mind...........Kid Dynamite ...........1976 ... Cream
Jam on the Groove...........Ralph MacDonald ...........1976 ... Marlin
Knock Him Out Sugar Ray...........Experience Unlimited ...........1980 ... Vermack
Blow Your Head ...........Fred Wesley & the J.B.s ...........1974 ... People

**SBR-515 (1987)**
Change (Makes You Want To Hustle) ...........Donald Byrd ...........1975 ... Blue Note
Brother Green (the Disco King) ...........Roy Ayers ...........1975 ... Polydor
* Mr. Magic...........Grover Washington Jr. ...........1975 ... CTI...........4:30 of the 9:11 LP version is used.
Main Theme from Star Wars...........David Matthews...........1977 ... CTI
* Jack and Diane...........John Cougar...........1982 ... Epic
* Bouncy Lady...........Pleasure ...........1975 ... Fantasy
Rock Music...........Jefferson Starship ...........1979 ... Grunt

**SBR-516 (1987)**
The Assembly Line ...........Commodores...........1974 ... Motown
I Walk on Guilded Splinters...........Johnny Jenkins...........1974 ... Capricorn
* Gimme What You Got ...........Le Pamplemousse...........1976 ... AVI ...........12-inch "Long" version
"T" Plays It Cool ...........Marvin Gaye ...........1972 ... Tamla
* Think (About It)...........Lyn Collins...........1972 ... People
* Space Dust...........Galactic Force Band ...........1978 ... Springboard
* Take the Money and Run ...........Steve Miller Band...........1976 ... Capitol

**SBR-517 (1987)**
Listen to Me...........Baby Huey...........1970 ... Curtom
* The Lovermaniacs (Sex) ...........Boobie Knight & the Universal Lady ...........1974 ... Dakar
Yes We Can Can ...........Pointer Sisters ...........1973 ... Blue Thumb
One Man Band (Plays All Alone) ...........Monk Higgins ...........1974 ... Buddha
N.T...........Kool & The Gang ...........1971 ... De-Lite ...............The final 3:19 of the 6:29 LP version is used (aka "N.T. Pt. 2" off the 45 version).
* Let a Woman Be a Woman, Let a Man Be a Man........Dyke & the Blazers ...........1969 ... Original Sound
Whiskey and Wine ...........Bram Tchaikovsky ...........1979 ... Radarscope ............Off the "Girl of My Dreams" single.
* Feel Good [edit]...........Fancy ...........1974 ... Big Tree ...............Listed as "L.L. Bonus Beats," it is actually a loop of Fancy's "Feel Good" beat on 45 rpm.

**SBR-518 (1988)**
Let's Have Some Fun ...........Bar-Kays ...........1977 ... Mercury
Conga...........Lafayette Afro Rock Band ...........1976 ... Makossa
Yellow Sunshine...........Yellow Sunshine ...........1973 ... Philly International

* Song has been edited/manipulated

| | | | | |
|---|---|---|---|---|
| * It's Just Begun | Jimmy Castor Bunch | 1972 | RCA | Louis Flores edits the intro to "Troglodyte" ("What we gonna do right here is go back…") onto the beginning of "Just Begun." |
| It's My Thing | Marva Whitney | 1969 | King | |
| I Believe in Music | Kay Gees | 1976 | Gang | |
| Ride Sally Ride | Dennis Coffey | 1972 | Sussex | |

**SBR-519 (1988)**

| | | | | |
|---|---|---|---|---|
| Rock Creek Park | Blackbyrds | 1975 | Fantasy | |
| I Get Lifted | K.C. & the Sunshine Band | 1975 | TK | |
| Cookies | Brother Soul | 1975 | Leo Mini | |
| Misdemeanor | Foster Sylvers | 1973 | MGM/Pride | |
| Bring It Here | Wild Sugar | 1981 | TSOB | |
| * Chicken Yellow | Miami | 1974 | Drive | |
| Put the Music Where Your Mouth Is | Olympic Runners | 1974 | London | |
| * Sport | Lightnin' Rod | 1973 | United Artists | |

**SBR-520 (1988)**

| | | | | |
|---|---|---|---|---|
| * Lonesome Cowboy | Roy Ayers | 1976 | Polydor | |
| Chinese Chicken | Duke Williams | 1973 | Capricorn | |
| * I'm Gonna Get You | Joe Quartermain | 1974 | GSF | |
| * Reach Out of the Darkness | Friend & Lover | 1973 | Verve Forecast | |
| House of Rising Funk | Chubukos | 1973 | Mainstream | Issued as a 45 under the Chubukos name, they were called Afrique on LP. |
| Hook and Sling (Part 1) | Eddie Bo | 1969 | Scram | |
| * Kissing My Love | Bill Withers | 1973 | Sussex | |

**SBR-521 (1989)**

| | | | | |
|---|---|---|---|---|
| Free Your Mind | The Politicans | 1972 | Hot Wax | |
| * Papa Was Too | Joe Tex | 1966 | Dial | |
| Hector | The Village Callers | 1968 | Rampart | |
| Devil with the Bust | Sound Experience | 1974 | Philly Groove | |
| Soul Pride | James Brown | 1969 | King | |
| * Cramp Your Style | All the People | 1972 | Blue Candle | |
| Shaft in Africa (Addis) | Johnny Pate | 1973 | ABC | Listed as "Shaft in Africa." |
| * I'm Gonna Love You Just a Little Bit More Baby | Barry White | 1973 | 20th Century | |
| * Dizzy [edit] | Tommy Roe | 1969 | ABC | Listed as "L.L. Bonus Beats #2," it is an edit/loop of the drum break from Tommy Roe's "Dizzy." |

**SBR-522 (1989)**

| | | | | |
|---|---|---|---|---|
| Woman | Barrabas | 1972 | RCA | |
| Corazon | Creative Source | 1974 | Sussex | |
| Save the World | Southside Movement | 1974 | Wand | |
| * The Grunt (part 1) | J.B.s | 1970 | People | |
| Do the Funky Penguin (part 2) | Rufus Thomas | 1972 | Stax | |
| * Dynamite (the Bomb) | Shotgun | 1977 | ABC | |
| * Films | Gary Numan | 1979 | Atco | |

**SBR-523 (1989)**

| | | | | |
|---|---|---|---|---|
| * The Breakdown (part 2) | Rufus Thomas | 1971 | Stax | |
| Country Cooking | Jim Dandy | 1975 | Chrysalis | |
| Joyous | Pleasure | 1977 | Fantasy | |
| * Get Out of My Life Woman | Solomon Burke | 1968 | Atlantic | |
| You Don't Know How Much I Love You | Alphonse Mouzon | 1974 | Blue Note | |
| Oh Honey | Delegation | 1977 | Shady Brook | |
| * The Easiest Way To Fall | Freda Payne | 1970 | Invictus | |

**SBR-524 (1990)**

| | | | | |
|---|---|---|---|---|
| Tramp | Lowell Fulson | 1966 | Kent | |
| (You) Got What I Need | Freddie Scott | 1968 | Shout | |
| You Can't Love Me if You Don't Respect Me | Lyn Collins | 1975 | Polydor | |
| Blind Alley | The Emotions | 1972 | Volt | |
| Expansions | Lonnie Liston Smith | 1975 | Flying Dutchman | Listed as "Expansions - Part I," this is 3:07 of the 6:04 LP track (part 1 of the 45). |
| * Hard to Handle | Otis Redding | 1968 | Atco | |
| You and Love Are the Same | The Grassroots | 1969 | Atco | |
| Sneakin' in the Back | Tom Scott | 1974 | Ode | |

**SBR-525 (1991)**

| | | | | |
|---|---|---|---|---|
| I've Been Watchin' You | Southside Movement | 1973 | Scepter | |
| Pot Belly | Lou Donaldson | 1970 | Blue Note | |
| Mambo #5 | Samba Soul | 1977 | RCA | 12-inch version |
| * Don't Change Your Love | Five Stairsteps | 1968 | Curtom | |
| Take Off Your Make Up | Lamont Dozier | 1973 | ABC | |
| Love & Affection | Ike White | 1976 | LA | |
| * The Payback | James Brown | 1973 | Polydor | |

* Song has been edited/manipulated

# AN APPRECIATION

I'd like to return to the classics. Perhaps the most famous classic in all the world of music, maybe the ultimate break of all: "Impeach the President." The original 45 rpm single was issued in 1973 by a small label called Alaga, based in Jamaica, Queens. The band is listed as "The Honey Drippers," with writing credits going to Johnson-Hammond, production by Roy C.

The lyrics of the song refer to the debate over Richard Nixon's impeachment. Whether the lyrics defend or denigrate the impeachment movement is unclear. About one thing, however, there can be no doubt: the popping soul-funk of the Honey Drippers band.

The Honey Drippers were a quartet comprised of a sax, guitar, bass, and drums, fronted by a man who modestly referred to himself as "cool, tall, good lookin'": Roy C. Hammond. Drummer Morris has the first four measures of the tune to himself, and makes the most of it with a beat that is one of the most recognizable and well-used breaks of all-time. As the crisp beat crackles like an electrical storm, we get a little rap from the bandleader. "Ladies and Jennamin," Roy begins, "we got the Honey Drippers in the house tonight. They just got back from Washington D.C. And I think they got something they want to say." Fred, the 6'1" bassist, doesn't disappoint with his contribution—a bouncy groove meshing with a guitar chop that prefigures developments in reggae. Roy breaks down the situation: "Some people say that he's guilty, some people say 'I don't know.'" The titular chorus storms through, leaving Roy to scold an impeachment-happy Honey Dripper with "Shut up, fool!" before he gets back into his rap. Reminding us that "behind the walls of the White House there's a lot of things we don't know about," he continues to drop political science over the effortlessly high-stepping funk.

It's a brilliant, simple, and masterful tune. Not a note out of place, and a groove your granny could get down too, even if she ain't a funky one. A novelty tune, sure, but one that had surprising resonance twenty-six years later, both lyrically and musically.

The flip side is entitled "Roy C's Theme," another likeable groove. This time Roy introduces the band, throwing us a few crumbs regarding the identities of the band members and letting us know that "they're all from New York City." The fate of the Honey Drippers band is obscure, (they never released an LP and had only one other 45; we don't even know their full names), but we do know that Roy C. Hammond graduated to the big leagues and had a successful career, mainly on the Mercury label, singing smooth R&B ballads.

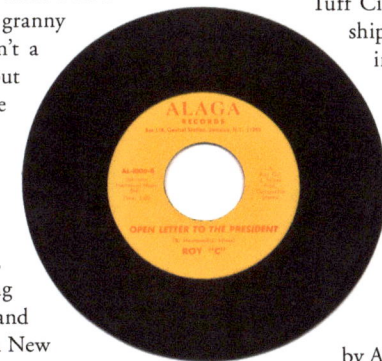

This beat, like many of the *Ultimate* breaks, has been used so many times it would be virtually impossible to list them all here. Hip-hop anthem "The Bridge" (Bridge, 1986) was based on a souped-up version of this rhythm, with Marley reworking Roy C's vocal intro ("Ladies and Gentlemen, you got MC Shan and Marley Marl in the house tonight..."). Like many others, Marley also isolated the kick and snare hits and programmed beats using them (see Biz Markie's "Make the Music..."). Another one of my favorites is Sammy B's live dissection of the bass/guitar groove for the Jungle Brothers' "Braggin' & Boastin'" (Warlock, 1987). EPMD has returned to this motherlode plenty of times; for example, layering the beat with BT Express to make "So Whatcha Sayin'?" (Fresh, 1989). Erick and Parrish also benefited from DJ Scratch doing his thing with Roy's vocal intro on their "Got to Give the People" (Def Jam, 1991). It sounds like Ced Gee used a sampled snare hit from "Impeach" for early BDP tracks as well. Another of the distinctive elements of this drum break is the beautifully clear open hi-hat sound, a tone that's distinguishable in the thickest multitracked collages.

"Impeach the President" is such an obscure and sought-after record that it has even been bootlegged as a 7-inch, complete with a replica yellow and red Alaga label. This track also has the dubious distinction of being owned by Tuff City, acquired in owner Aaron Fuchs's buying spree of classic break records. A regretful Roy C. has unsuccessfully attempted to regain his signed-away publishing rights, and Tuff City refuses to comment on its relationship with the label. Through Tuff City's involvement, this obscure 45-only release was reissued as a nationally distributed 12-inch single, complete with "Bonus Beats"—for the crossfader impaired, I suppose. Strangely enough, the first glimpse I ever had of the original Alaga label was back in 1989 on the cover of the 45 Kingdom LP by Mark the 45 King—a record published by... Tuff City. ◉

by Andrew Mason

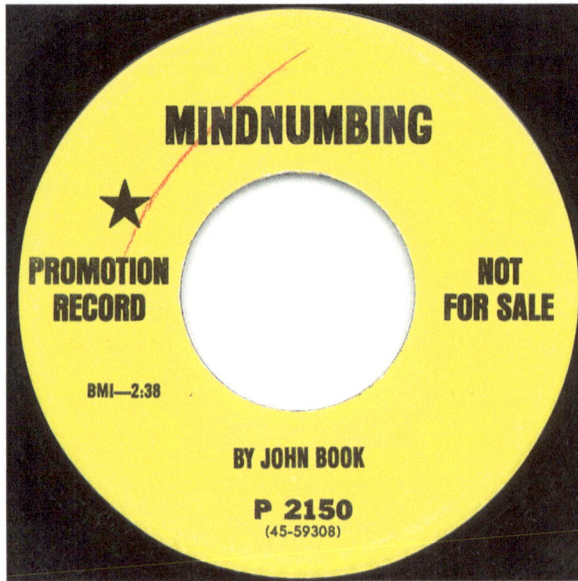

MINDNUMBING

PROMOTION
RECORD

NOT
FOR SALE

BMI—2:38

BY JOHN BOOK

P 2150
(45-59308)

In the winter of 1999, Mark Herlihy asked Cut Chemist and DJ Shadow to take part in the Future Primitive Sound-sessions in San Francisco—a series of performances where DJs could go at it one-on-one in the spirit of creating and showcasing good music. It was heard that both DJs would take things one step further and conduct their routines using 45 rpm records, helping to create a buzz for the performance itself.

After their set, DJ Shadow threw some 45s into the crowd, including a copy of Funka Fize's "Because You're Funky." When he signed a Future Primitive poster for the fan who caught his 45, Shadow told him, "I shouldn't have thrown that record out; I might have to use it sometime in the future"—unknowingly foreshadowing the events to come.

It was assumed that Future Primitive would eventually release a legitimate version of this musical union, following the success of the Cut Chemist and Shortkut CD. But only a lo-fi bootleg surfaced. Word leaked out that a "secret recording" was made the night before the actual performance, with the two DJs doing practice runs of the routine; it had been recorded on DAT, thus the quality was superb. It happened to be true.

Only 1,000 copies were initially pressed—a fifty-five-minute megamix of old soul and funk 45s, mixed in with radio spots and the occasional hip-hop record. Its semi-official, semi-bootleg look (right down to the Italian warning label similar to those peculiar funk compilations coming out of Italy) added to the recording's mystique, as many were confused as to its origins.

Little did most fans know, the duo had pressed the CDs themselves and Cut Chemist had sold them while on tour.

Later he had put a few CDs up for sale at a Los Angeles record store—only for someone to buy and sell them on eBay. It forced Cut Chemist and DJ Shadow to react by posting notices on eBay, urging fans not to pay ridiculous prices. But it was too late, as prices would continue to escalate, and fans would continue to pay. Another 1,000 copies were pressed, which DJ Shadow sold on his Goodwill tour in the Fall of 1999.

Multiple copies of *Brainfreeze* began showing up on eBay. "Rare," "Out of Print," "Limited Edition": phrases placed upon a new compact disc that would sell on the auction site as if it was rare vinyl—$60, $80, and higher. It soon became obvious that the CD, itself non-legit, had been bootlegged. Even an LP surfaced. Fans began inquiring about and, due to a sickness known as *collecting*, searching for the "original" CDs.

As it became clear how futile and irrelevant and unsatisfying this search was, people turned to locating the original recordings from the *Brainfreeze* CD. This, of course, became the biggest part of the phenomenon, not only among the crate-digging elite but also for fans who may not have entered a thrift store or dingy basement in their lives. A DJ Shadow sample site pushed things forward, issuing a close-to-definitive list. Little records that once went for $3 or so skyrocketed to the triple-digit region when placed on eBay. These 45s, once the little secrets of funk collectors, became not only in high-demand but also common knowledge.

Wax Poetics contributing writer Oliver Wang says the craze for hunting down funk records wasn't new, since "there was already a growing awareness and compiling of those rarities." Wang continues, "I don't think anyone knew it would blow up the way that it did—you can never predict that kind of thing—but it makes total sense. But I don't think it necessarily created a craze in funk 45s—it helped bring it to light, but the seeds had already been planted."

Phill Stroman, better known as Soulman, wasn't sure what to expect when he first heard of the CD. The Internet had been the breeding ground for much of the hype, and he didn't think the recording would live up to expectations. "I had to admit that it far exceeded whatever I thought it might be," Soulman says. "The selection of 45s, rare and common, was really nice and the scratching was on point. But I think I was most impressed by the fact that it was all done live, not tracked up and overdubbed. That was the most impressive thing when you look at the complexity of how it was all put together. I'd always felt that the approach towards doing a beat tape should be that it's a produced piece of work, not just a DJ mix put on tape. So what Cut and Shadow did, they gave you the best of both worlds: a totally live mix showing DJ skills but with complex production values as well." Soulman would eventually do two tracks on his own CD dedicated to "Frozen Heads," making his own *Brainfreeze*-style megamixes and flipping some of the records used in the routine.

But, Soulman says, these types of mixes have been done before, and *Brainfreeze*'s popularity may have been due to one obvious thing. "I don't mean this as a knock on Cut or Shadow, but the truth is that whenever a white dude does something that Black people originated, and is actually dope with it, they're gonna get blown up even bigger. You can call it the Elvis/Eminem factor, and add all the others that have come in between those two. This is not Cut or Shadow's fault, they're just trying to do some dope shit. But the fans and the media are always looking for the next great white hope, and in a sense this is a continuation of what's been going on forever, and I think it's one reason why *Brainfreeze* has been as big as it has."

For some, the CD could be the "Lesson #5" DJ Shadow and Cut Chemist had always promised to do. But whatever your reason for getting into the *Brainfreeze* experience, it was a CD that helped wrap up another decade of record collecting, crate-digging, musical discoveries, and most importantly, hip-hop. *Brainfreeze* may not have been the starting point, but its placement in the marketplace came off like an Alka-Seltzer in a seagull's belly. Its aftershocks, good or bad, is still being felt years after the fact.

Here is a look at some of the parts that make up the *Brainfreeze* whole.

### THUNDER KICK INTRO

*Brainfreeze* helped bring attention to radio spots—records sent to radio stations to promote the latest movies and television shows. Outside of well-known artists, though, most radio spots would collect dust. In the intro, the duo spun the *Thunder Kick* radio spot, and scratched "Also Sprach

Zarathustra" by the Spacemen (Blowfly's band). "[It's] the kind of shit that you just don't hear anybody else doing these days," Soulman comments. "Although it did bring back memories of the kind of shit that Afrika Islam was doing twenty years ago on the 'Zulu Beats' show on WHBI in New York."

### REUBEN BELL
"Superjock" (Alarm III)

How could you resist a record that featured the lyrics, "He's number one/He's the turntable king"? Reuben Bell was a part of the soul scene in Shreveport, Louisiana, releasing records on Murco before finding himself on a number of other labels. "Super Jock" is the B-side to "I Still Have to Say Goodbye." But "Superjock" is U.S.-only, as there is a different B-side song on the U.K. 45 on Contempo Records.

### EDDIE BO & INEZ CHEATHAM
"Lover and a Friend" (Capitol P-2057; 1967)

This record by Eddie Bo and Mary Jane Hooper (credited as "Inez Cheatham") was originally released on the New Orleans-based Seven-B label before Capitol picked it up for national distribution. The beat was sampled in '93 on Luscious Jackson's "Keep on Rockin'" from their debut ep, *In Search of Manny*. Following *Brainfreeze*, the beat has been heard in television commercials from United Parcel Service to Tampax, and is even the basis of the theme song to the syndicated TV show *Blind Date*.

### MYSTIC MOODS
"Cosmic Sea" (Warner Bros. WB-7686)

Brad Miller—known amongst audiophiles as the founder of the Mobile Fidelity Sound Lab record label—created the Mystic Moods Orchestra. The music was arguably lightweight but would occasionally have shining moments. Miller had a thing for trains, rain, and other sound effects, and went out of his way to add them to his music. During the '70s, Mystic Moods gained a more contemporary sound with the help of some well-known session musicians. 1973 produced "Cosmic Sea," a nice funky track with orchestration and thick keys. Miller was very peculiar about what songs of his went where, and that included the different vinyl formats. If you want the version used on *Brainfreeze*, you have to buy the 45, as the edits are slightly different than that of the stereo and quadraphonic LPs. The white label 45, seen inside the *Brainfreeze* CD booklet, is also worth looking for, as the mono version of the song (meant for airplay on AM radio stations) has a completely different mix as well.

## SIMTEC & WYLIE
"Bootleggin' (Part 2)" (Mister Chand CH-8009)

When Gene Chandler's career was slowing down, Mercury Records gave him his own custom label. One of his first acts was Simtec & Wylie, a vocal duo in the style of Sam & Dave. Their voices were very strong, and each would eventually go on to their own solo careers. One of their more popular songs was "Bootleggin'"—not about illegal pressings of vinyl but some promiscuous sexual activity. The song was made famous by Pete Rock as the intro and outro to the classic "Straighten It Out" with CL Smooth.

## THE SHOWMEN INC.
"The Tramp (from Funky Broadway) (Part 1)" (Now N-3)

A solid 45 with some of the nicest breaks around. While it can be located on funk compilations, you'll want to search for the 45 just to hear Part 2, where the singer sings to the point of exhaustion.

## PLEASURE WEB
"Music Man Part 1 & 2" (Eastbound E-617)

The source of the flute solo in Jurassic 5's "Jayou" had been unknown by all but the elite vinyl junkies (some guessed wrongly that it was an obscure cover of Bob Marley's "Get Up Stand Up"). But when J5 was signed to Interscope they were forced to give up the source of the sample, and the search was on by beatdiggers to find this Pleasure Web 45.

While most are familiar with Westbound Records, Eastbound's history is a unique one in itself. Created by Armen Boladian as a daring side to Westbound, Eastbound would develop artists on the jazzier side of things. The actual identity of Pleasure Web is unknown, but rumor has it that the Ohio Players cut this record during the *Pleasure* sessions. Jesse McDaniel and Clarence Williams are credited as songwriters, with Jesse getting a shoutout in the song itself. This 1973 record, along with Third Guitar's "Baby Don't Cry" and Tony Alvon & the Belairs' "Sexy Coffee Pot," is one of the rarest pieces used on *Brainfreeze*.

## GARY BYRD
"Soul Travelin' (The G.B.E.) (Part 1)" (RCA DJHQ-0048)

Backed by the Jimmy Castor Bunch, Byrd talks his way through this song, introducing the world to various soul music hot spots, from Detroit to Los Angeles to Memphis. The intro was sampled by producer Jazzie B. on Soul II Soul's "Jazzie's Groove." You'll want to also hunt down the stock 45 with

Part 2, where Byrd and Castor take a playful jab at the Castor Bunch.

## FUNKA FIZE
"Because You're Funky"/"No Words" (Royce 1000)

This rare 45 was produced by George Kerr, the soul singer-turned-writer/producer who also worked with the Skull Snaps and the Whatnauts. He later brought his expertise to Sugar Hill Records. Kerr sued Naughty By Nature for breach of contract.

## STU GARDNER AND THE SANCTIFIED SOUND
*S/T* (Volt VOS-0503)

Bill Cosby discovered Stu Gardner and helped him get a contract with Volt Records. When Gardner's popularity fell, Cosby brought him on as musical director for *The Cosby Show* on NBC. He now does the music for Nickelodeon's *Little Bill* cartoon series.

Gardner's self-titled album is one of the few LPs used on *Brainfreeze*. Cut Chemist had used the second break in "Devil in a Man" as part of his remix of DJ Shadow's "The Number Song," which was expanded in the *Brainfreeze* routine.

## SAMSON & DELILAH AND THE BOSS CITY PEOPLE
"There's a DJ in Your Town" (Indigo IN-315)

A nice, late-'60s funk track in the vein of Sly & the Family Stone's "Dance to the Music"—each member is introduced by the instrument he plays. After the introductory organ solo, the vocalist raps about the disc jockey being a major part of every city. The song eventually moves to a nice drum break, then goes into some chicken scratch guitar before the singers reference Sly once again, through singing the hook from "Sing a Simple Song." The record would eventually be released on the Black Prince label, with a similar catalog number. DJ Shadow found it years later, sampling some vocals ("play that funky solo") on "Organ Donor." ◐

*John Book is a record collector from Washington State who produces music under the name of Crut. Book also maintains a number of fan-based music websites, including those for Ozomatli, Prince Paul, and Wu-Tang Clan. He is currently a contributing writer for the online publication* Funkier Than Thou.

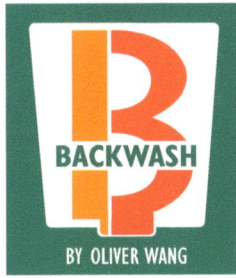

First came *Brainfreeze*. Then came the inevitable bootlegs. Now witness the compilations. The logic is obvious—if *BF* is built off of rare 45s, why not make a comp of the full-length songs? The result has been (so far) four different series that have sought to capitalize on *BF*. And while we here at WAX POETICS frown upon the profiteering of compilation practices (yeah right), as a public service, we're providing a guide to sorting out the best of the bunch.

## THE CRITERIA

**Bite Marks**–How bad did they bite *BF*; to what lengths would they shamelessly capitalize? Self-explanatory.

**Chill Index**–How good is the song selection; do they offer the best off of *BF*? The trick here is not just to rock the best songs, but also to be the only ones doing it. At this point, "Dance the Slurp" is everywhere, but do you have the ultra-rare "Quit Jive' In" by Pearly Queen? Or Reuben Bell's stunning "Superjock"? The harder your cuts, the colder your rating.

## THE RECORDS

*New York Convention Breaks Vol. 1* (2000)–The oldest of the comps, the main thing that gives this away as *BF*-related is the presence of "Dance the Slurp." Mack Rice's "Three People in Love," another *BF* song shows up, as does Giorgio's haunting "Tears." But the rest of the selections, including a scintillating cover of the Mohawks' "Champ," ("Tramp" by Brother Lloyd's All Stars) and an interesting but uneven cover of "Superstition" by Japan's Goro are not *BF*-based.

**Bite Marks:** Indention

**Chill Index:** Lukewarm–Of the ten songs, only "Tramp" and John Schroeder's heavy "Headband" are really worth having.

*Dance the Slurp* (2001)–This sixteen-song series from the U.K., on two separately sold records (one with a red cover, the other white), seems like a wack knock-off with its cheap artwork—plus the hefty import prices may not make them seem worth it. But once you actually look at the song selection, it's definitely got some strong *BF* assets. It's the only *BF* comp on vinyl that includes the Interpretations' "Jason Pew Mosso," Ultimate Force's raucous "I'm Not Playin," and Pearly Queen's "Quit Jive' In." And might be the only comp anywhere to have American Gypsy's "Inside Out" and Samson & Delilah's "There's a DJ in Your Town." At the same time, it still repeats tracks that had been comped earlier, like the Vibrettes' "Humpty Dump," Third Guitar's "Baby Don't Cry," and Lou Courtney's "Hey Joyce."

**Bite Marks:** Puncture

**Chill Index:** Brisk–If they didn't cost so much, they'd be chiller.

*Brainfreeze Breaks* (2001)–The only comp exclusively on CD, the artwork is obviously *BF*-inspired though the cover photograph is beyond dull. However, there's no faulting the generosity—twenty-plus tracks deep, longer than any other comp out there. This volume helps balance out weaker/common inclusions—such as the ubiquitous "Keep On Dancing" and Gary Byrd's goofy "Soul Travelin'"—with the stronger ones—Salt's hunk of funk, "Hung Up," the Nu People's breakbeat badness of "I'd Be Nowhere Without You," along with "Superjock" and "Quit Jive' In." It's also the only comp in the group that has tough funk 45 songs like the Soul Lifters' "Hot, Funky and Sweaty," and "Soul Brother Testify" by the Original Soul Senders. There's a good deal of material here that is available elsewhere (Wilbur Bascomb's "Just a Groove in 'G'" for example) but overall, there's little flat fare on here.

**Bite Marks:** Laceration

**Chill Index:** Frosty–Comprehensive, yes, but making it CD-only is a no-no for breakheads.

*Slurped* (2001)–Appearing with masks pulled over their face (yeah, that's right, hide yourselves, you pirates), whoever made this comp deserves points just for moxy alone: they straight jacked the visual elements *BF*'s original artwork, even down to the kind of photo stock used by B+. Beyond that though, this sixteen-song, double LP (also on CD) has all the goodies that most would want from a *BF* comp: Nu-People, Salt, Reuben Bell, "Lover and a Friend" by Eddie Bo, Fried Chicken's "Funky DJ," et al. And though you can find other songs like Marlena Shaw's "California Soul" and Rufus Thomas's "Itch and Scratch" elsewhere, they hardly detract from the comp's worth.

**Bite Marks:** Amputation

**Chill Index:** Cold as Ice–It may not have the most songs or even the absolute rarest, but *Slurped*'s combination of selection and pricing is unmatched—so far. ◉

# Cut Chemist and DJ Shadow: Funk Soul Brothers

by Oliver Wang

Depending on your point of view, you can either laud or blame DJ Shadow and Cut Chemist for sparking off the funk 45 phenomenon. While they were hardly the first to bring 45s to international attention, 1999's *Brainfreeze* album and tour helped promote the fascination—and frenzy—over funk 7-inches to heretofore-unforeseen heights. In late 2001, they did it again, following up *Brainfreeze* with the even more ambitious *Product Placement*. Wax Poetics's Oliver Wang sat down with hip-hop's new audio two in October, forty-eight hours before they launched the *Product Placement* tour at San Francisco's famed Fillmore.

**How's the new show coming together?**

**Cut Chemist:** It's shaping up. It's tough… we're pretty much trying to do eight of [the L.A. *Brainfreeze* show], and that [show] was pretty tough, looking back on it, trying to get all the little video game things and stuff like that going on.

We got videos, CDs, shirts, posters—it's like doing a job of a corporation here.

**How is *Product Placement* different from *Brainfreeze*?**

**DJ Shadow:** Twice as many records, twice as much fun, twice as much Vitamin D for your dollar. We're working twice as hard. We got a good compliment from our tour manager the other day who sat through part of the set when we were rehearsing. He was like, "Yeah, you really managed to…[take] it to another level but still [make] it fun like *Brainfreeze*."

**To what degree does the rarity of the selection factor in?**

**CC:** Well, I don't have any rare records. I'm the one who put "Keep on Dancing" on the first one. [*laughter*]

**And Alvin Cash thanks you for it.**

**CC:** It's pretty much what sounds good. On this one, there's a side of me that thinks all the deep funk, heavy, rare guys are going to be checking for it, like, "Let's see what he put on this next one." They'll probably be looking for those kind of songs on this one. But really, it's what sounds good and it's the same formula.

**DJS:** What sounds good always wins.

**CC:** It's always timeless. When those records aren't interesting to people anymore, then where does it leave the product itself?

The blends are just—they're off the hook. We play a lot less of a lot of records. We're just gunning through records left and right.

**DJS:** The thing I'm starting to realize is that I'm going to mess up at least one time and that's okay. I think I would anyway. It's so close on some of the transitions—I catch it once every two or three times.

**CC:** If your records aren't placed right, you're done, forget it. It's like playing chess; you have to think four records ahead of the one you're playing, otherwise, forget about it.

**How did you pick what sets would make the final cut?**

**DJS:** We would [practice] until we messed up really badly, until everything came to a screeching halt. Then we'd go again, another ten minutes, and then we did it all the way through a couple of times and basically took the best portions. There's still mistakes on the CD, there's still some limp-wristed scratches and a lot of places where you can hear us pushing the records. We didn't want it to be like: stop every three seconds or stop at every transition.

**CC:** Or real stale sounding, like almost tracked. There has to be that human element, like on *Brainfreeze*. I think one of the things that I hear most about *Brainfreeze* is, "Man, that wasn't perfect, I hear flaws in it…"

**DJS:** Or: "…I got all those records." As far as that whole rarity thing, there's always going to be people who totally miss the point and be like, "Oh man…I got all those records, how come nobody likes my DJing?" Or whatever—that's not the point. Rarity is the least.

**I know both of you are kind of sick of talking about this but I have to: Looking back on *Brainfreeze*, did you really expect the hype that surrounded it?**

**CC:** I didn't. When we did the show for Mark Herlihy, I said, "Let's tape the set, just for reference." We listened to it—I was listening to it in my car, over and over again. I said, "Hey, this is kind of cool." [Shadow] said the same thing. I thought, "Why don't we just press up a thousand? I'm going to be going on tour, maybe I can sell it on tour." Next thing you know, I put ten in Aron's Records [in L.A.] and I think that's where the whole thing started. Some guy picked them up and started selling them on eBay and then it snowballed from there.

**Drama and all, how do you feel about the whole affair?**

**DJS:** I can just say for my point of view, it's been really a valuable outlet for me because at the time of [*Brainfreeze*] I wasn't ready to do an album yet because I had just finished working on [*Psyence Fiction*]. I just was in this kind of mode where I knew I wanted to be on the road, and that was cool. I was looking for something else to do. It was just kind of organic, the way it came about. And just so directly down the line of what my interests were, and what could be better? To get to be DJing, listening to music, collecting…

**CC:** He said during a practice session, "Thanks for mixing my two greatest loves: mixing and 45s."

**DJS:** Exactly. Every time we do this set, I'm just up there smiling the whole time. Still, to this day, working on this set that people haven't heard yet, I start cracking up, thinking about what people's reactions are going to be or if they're going to be distraught or dismayed or amused or bemused.

So, I think, after we did some [*Brainfreeze* shows] on the road, and [even] after the whole episode with the records being stolen…and everything—I [was] definitely hoping that we could do it again. These sort of outlets, whether it's this or Quannum or my album, it's all so important and equally so. Different facets that are available to me personally to manifest my love for music—this is just something that is so dope to me. ◗

*Oliver Wang writes on music and culture for the SF Bay Guardian, L.A. Weekly, URB, The Source, and other publications. He also hosts a weekly radio show in Berkeley, CA. On his website o-dub.com, he regularly reviews both new music as well as stuff dug out of the crates.*

# MR. SUPREME
# UNEARTHED

Interview by Phill Stroman
Photos by Karla Clark

I first interviewed Seattle's Mr. Supreme back in 1994 for *Rap Sheet* after he sent me an impressive top ten list of "Beats to Catch"—stuff that was at the time light years ahead of what others were sending me. In the years following, Supreme hit me with a bunch of tapes that confirmed the obvious—the man is one of the leading break experts on the planet. A nice assortment of underground records on his own Conception Records, along with five Conmen break CDs recorded with partner Jake One, further cemented his rep as King of the Beats.

Fast forward to 2001 and we see that Preme is still diggin' and still building on his legendary status in the crates community. There have been ups and downs, drama and turmoil along the way but through it all he's still standing and ready to reach for new heights. You think you know but you have no idea.

**SOULMAN:** It's been a while since that *Rap Sheet* interview in '94. What's happened and what's changed in your life in the past seven years?

**MR. SUPREME:** Wow, has it been that long already? I guess time flies when you're having fun! Basically, if you remember, I was gearing up to start my label at that time. I actually started it a few years after that, as I was doing freelance stuff for other labels, Columbia, EMI, WEA, and a lot of independents as well. Then I started Conception and made it my full time gig along with DJing.

The major thing that changed my life was that I got a divorce within this time. It was really hard around that time as my father had passed away and our parent label Sub Pop [yes, the rock label] decided they didn't want to back us any longer. So it was like three majorly heavy things being dropped on me all at once. I was very depressed to say the least. I had just moved into this really nice house with my wife and after we were there for two weeks she dropped the bomb on me. So I had to leave with nothing but my records and start all over again. I was actually homeless for about a month. I was sleeping wherever I could. I always had the couch at my dukes' crib, but it just wasn't right. I stacked some chips and pretty much bought the first condo I looked at! I should have looked around some more but I needed something. I'm still living there to this day. My depression lasted for a whole year!

Oh yeah, I also had two partners that were running the label with me. At around this same time one of them decided to leave as he didn't get along with the other partner. There was tension in the offices everyday and shit was just fucked up. So it was me and my other partner—he calls me up one day and says let's go out for lunch tomorrow. So the next day we are sitting there getting our grub on when he pulls out this paper explaining to me that we are going to close the office and sell our studio because he has decided to move to NYC! I was like, "Oh, so because you decided to leave we are supposed to do this? Nigga, please!" He left for NYC and I kept the label going. We had no dough and no distributor! I was paying out of my own pocket to keep the shit going.

I knew we could get some distribution somewhere so I went to California and struck an agreement with Nu Gruv. My man Nu Mark from Jurassic 5 had suggested them to me since they did such a great job with the Jurassic ep. They knew our stuff and who I was and it was on! [But] like every new relationship it started out great and ended up sour. If you notice, all the good labels that were distributed by Nu Gruv (Conception, Stones Throw, Ill Boogie) have left them! Now what does that tell you? Shit, my man Peanut Butter Wolf used to work there and he still left! So now I'm back to square one after all this time and seems like I'm starting out all over again.

Anyways, back to my one year depression. I woke up one day and I don't know what happened but I was finally over everything. That entire year all I did was DJ and try to keep the label going. I had a gig that night and when I was at the club I noticed all these fly ass honies in the spot. The funny thing is, the past year I didn't notice shit. I would go to my gigs and not really talk to anyone and just DJ, get my cash, and bounce. This night was different. I was noticing all kinds of shit. So I started kicking game to these chicks and they were having it! Some of us exchanged numbers and I eventually ended up with some of them. That was about three years ago. It seems as [if] I haven't stopped noticing shit and taking advantage of my opportunities. So here's the kicker! For some odd unknown reason it seems like most of the chicks I meet or end up hanging out with are escorts, strippers, or porn stars! So I'm becoming friends with all these freaks, and they're telling me, "Daddy, let's make a movie!" What am I supposed to do? These chicks are like, "You already make records, so just do a movie too and put some music to that shit and make it fly." So I've ended up attending the AVN awards [the Oscars of the porn industry] the last two years and just being around all kinds of fly shit. So I look back at the last seven years and if I was still married none of this would be happening! I'm getting paid to travel around the world, kick it in clubs, kick it with porno stars, look for records, and stay in nice hotels! How long is this dream going to last? Oh, next question!

**SM:** Well, before we go to that next question, how exactly are you getting paid to travel, stay in nice hotels, etc.? If it's some down low pimp shit that you'd rather not go into detail about, we understand. But we are curious!

**MS:** Oh, no don't get it twisted! I leave that up to the Bishop Don Magic Juan and Mr. White Folks. I DJ a lot everywhere I can. I don't have a manager or even a booking agent; so far I have done it on my own and word of mouth. I remember DJing in an ice hockey arena up in Canada for Run-DMC. Vegas, Germany, all over. So all you promoters out there don't be afraid to bring me out to rock one night at your club, party, fashion show, orgy, or whatever!

**SM:** What's the status of Conception Records right now?

**MS:** On the real, I feel like we never even had a label and we are at square one! I'm still running it solo with the help of a few interns. We left our distributor but I do have some options. I got some sick shit in the works, B. We are far from dead! Most of our artists have left the label. I'm not the type to try to hold anyone down and especially anyone in my family. If you're on my label, then you're family. The fucked up thing is that business can really ruin friendships. It's not even business but money. You have read it time and time again forever and it's true. These cats feel like they should be millionaires or something. They don't even realize that their records didn't even recoup initial expenses! They think because they went to the store and seen their record or because they read about it in a magazine they are selling millions of copies. In the meantime the fucking distributors aren't paying us and we are going broke. I still owe our graphic artists a grip.

**SM:** Yeah, those fuckin' distributors, man. Some dudes owe me money, too.

**MS:** Then we got the jealous artist that thinks we didn't push their record as hard as we did another. So running a label is a real headache. Then on top of that, once you start to do well or start being noticed, the lawsuits start coming in. It's like fucking Bill Gates and Microsoft. That cat is untouchable. The government had to come in and try to break up his company. That was some bullshit. Let the man ball out of control! Isn't that what America prides itself on?

So, we are still in effect. A lot of the artists and producers we had are doing shit for major labels now! So this is the kind of shit I'm working with. Every one knows it. We got emails everyday from around the world telling us how dope our shit is. Our records are being sampled by major artists! This is for real, I'm not joking. In the meantime I'm out here struggling to keep my shit going. If I had the backing to do videos, etc., it's guaranteed that we would be an urban powerhouse. I'm trying to work on a deal with a major at the moment. I don't know what it's going to take to do this shit. I see so much bullshit coming out on major labels with videos, print ads, and the whole nine. I have been DJing for seventeen years and I still am! I know what it takes to rock clubs, airwaves, etc. I should really be holding down an A&R position somewhere. So we are still here with some shit in the works and if you haven't heard of us yet, check out our web page at conceptionrecords.net and buy some of our stuff.

**SM:** What have you learned in your experience running an indie label, and what advice would you give to those who are thinking about starting a label of their own?

**MS:** First off, it isn't easy. I would say start with having a great distribution chain. That is key. Lots of capital to work with, a fabulous lawyer, and, finally, excellent product.

**SM:** Which of your releases on Conception was your favorite? I personally liked a lot of the joints but I'm partial to that Grassroots LP, which, as I've told you before, I think people are gonna be diggin' for and paying top dollar for twenty years from now.

**MS:** No doubt! That record is classic, man. I'm a big fan of Da Grassroots. The reason people are gonna be paying top dollar is because it's going to take time to get out there and for people to start hearing about it. That is because it didn't get the push it should have. We are a very small label with a shoestring budget. It just didn't get promoted right. That is easily a gold album. No question. I don't even think *The Source* reviewed it. I sent it to every publication and the reviews were limited. It doesn't even matter now if the record is dope or not. I'm sure if we did a double spread ad campaign we could have had a review or an interview. Another thing is that people want to sleep on shit and basically judge a book by it's cover! When they see Seattle, Washington, on the record, they automatically think it's going to be wack.

**SM:** So what's up with the record collection? By now you must have what, 50,000 records? Are you running out of storage space yet?

**MS:** Yes I am. My uno bedroom condo has filled up fast. I actually think I only have about 20,000 records. Then I got my couch, TV, turntables, etc. There is not much space at all. I do have a storage unit I rent that is full of records.

**SM:** What does the record collector who has everything dig for nowadays?

**MS:** I don't know. I guess I would have track one down and ask him! Well, hanging with Biz Markie and Cash Money, they got me into stupid shit! Like, the Huggy Bear doll from *Starsky & Hutch*. How could I resist owning a little pimp doll! That shit is bananas. I got Rock'em Sock'em Robots, the J.J. doll, Flip Wilson, Mr. T, Fat Albert lunch box, Speak & Spell. I got this ill board game called Feel

for a record. Don't think that I don't or haven't done that. It used to make my entire week when I found something I wanted. Now I just get it and make sure it's mint. I then put it in a plastic sleeve, throw it on the shelf and mark it off the list and go on to the next, poker-faced with absolutely no emotion!

**SM:** Do you still find stores that have anything worthwhile, or have you found some new ways to come across those rare collectibles? Yes, we want you to reveal all of your secrets!

**MS:** I try to travel as much as possible and to be honest every town in the USA is pretty much dried up! You see the same bullshit Firestone X-mas records every-fuckin'-where. There are some places that are cool though. The Bay Area is good or was the last time I was there. You have specialty shops that are decent, like Groove Merchant, Sound Library, A-1. These guys put in work and have good

## The men will literally lose sleep, disregard their hygiene, forget to eat, pass on sex, spend their life savings, and travel the world. All for a fucking record!

the Soul. You pick a card and it will say some shit like, "Your rap is strong, but your cash ain't long," then you lose five spaces. Original blaxploitation movie posters, kung fu movie posters, kung fu flicks, blaxploitation flicks, velvet paintings of nude soul sisters. I got the original copy of the 1974 *Players* magazine with the Pam Grier spread. I got these little Latin gangster figures called Homies, video games, *Good Times* trading cards, porno flicks, Jackson 5 cartoons on video, original episodes of *Soul Train*, James Brown on the *Mike Douglas Show*, portable turntables, and all kinds of fly shit.

**SM:** As one of the top beat collectors in the world, what would you say separates the men from the boys when it comes to collecting rare records?

**MS:** The men will literally lose sleep, disregard their hygiene, forget to eat, pass on sex, spend their life savings, and travel the world. All for a fucking record! The boys will just go out to the store, look around for about twenty minutes (only in the soul section), leave Stark Reality there because it cost $15 which is waaayyy too much, and not go back for a month or so. They will then get on eBay and buy Rita Jean Bodine for $50 because it says there is a break on it. (True stories by the way.)

**SM:** Is it important to you to find stuff at cheap prices, or is it just as satisfying to pay a lot just as long as you cop that record that you've coveted for years?

**MS:** Well, any true digger knows that if you put in the work you will find some real gems at a fraction of their market value. However, some records just weren't available in certain parts of the world and you will probably never find them. If you do, it will take your lifetime! So sometimes you just have to shell out that paper. It's not satisfying to me at all to shell out an absurd amount of money

shit. It almost makes sense to just save your dough for a year that you would spend on records and just go hit these spots up. They have already done all the digging and hard work for you. Although that is part of the fun if you have the time. Another good idea is to just run an ad in the local paper that you buy record collections. You'll get a lot of calls and go through millions of bullshit records, but you'll also come home with some gems.

**SM:** What do you think of this whole funk 45 movement that seems to be happening now, with everybody spending wildly to snap up funk tunes on 7-inch vinyl and bidding like crazy on eBay?

**MS:** It's just crazy, man. Why weren't these same guys buying these five or ten years back? I remember $50 was like stupid high for a 45 rpm. These records are going for an absurd amount of money. Way more than albums! I have been victim to this as well because there were a few titles I needed lately and had to pay dumb loot. I usually end up trading with these guys though. They want shit too! So it doesn't hit the bank too hard. I remember finding three copies of Tony Alvon & the Belairs "Sexy Coffee Pot" 7-inch last year. The guy wanted $75 each so I left them there. The last one I seen on eBay went for $550!

**SM:** A lot of people speak very negatively of eBay and the high prices that records go for in their auctions. What's your view on eBay, would you call it a good thing or a bad thing?

**MS:** I think it's both. I have paid many bills with eBay and thanks to them I will never ever be broke again in my lifetime! I have also scored some great shit I needed. Some high and some low. The only downfall is you have a lot of these jealous toys on there buying shit they know nothing about and really don't deserve it for not doing their homework. But hey, it's America and to each his own.

**SM:** Aside from eBay, how about digging online at various used record websites? Is this as valid a way to dig as actually going to spots and getting your fingertips cruddy?

**MS:** It's valid if you know what record you want and what's on it. Nothing compares to going out though finding that record no one has ever heard of and there is some shit on it.

**SM:** Diggin' itself seems to be growing in popularity by the moment. Seems like damn near everybody's diggin' for beats these days. Do you think it's a fad or something that's here to stay?

or something. Clearly he is wired when you go into his store. The problem I have with him is that I have been going in there for seventeen years. I have spent thousands of dollars with him and brought him numerous customers from around the world. He now tries to charge me the most outrageous fucking prices for shit just because it's me! He thinks it must be expensive if I want it. Nothing in his store is priced. He will tell you when you bring it up to the counter. I used to go in and grab what I wanted and hide the shit. Then a few days later I would send in my aunt or someone else to get the records. He would always charge them $10 and under for each title. For the same stack, if I brought them to the counter [the prices] would start at $35! And remember I had been going there for years and really

**MS:** It's a fad to a lot of people. However, there are the diehards like us and I already know I'm going to be just like the guy on the cover of your last CD. I will never stop diggin'. I see these kids out now days in stores and by luck they might pull something I need. I'll tell them, hey, do you want to trade that to me or let me get that? Then just because it's me asking they really want to keep it and think it's something special and tell me no way! They think they have something up on me! First of all this isn't a contest to have something that Mr. Supreme doesn't! That's what the toys around my way are doing. So I simply let them know that in a year or two or even five when they aren't doing it no more and they are on to the next fad to contact me as I will still be doing it and I will buy their collection from them! It really pisses them off, but I'm just stating the facts.

**SM:** Do you find yourself passing up records with generic drum breaks nowadays, or do you still have that "I-want-every-break-known-to-man" mentality that many of us in the crate digging world have?

**MS:** That's hilarious because I go into these modes where I'm like take or leave it, it's just another beat. Then I'll be on some shit where I'm like, *I must have every beat*! It goes back and forth like a Cameo song.

**SM:** Are there things about digging and record collecting that really piss you off?

**MS:** Yeah, you know, there is the one asshole dealer out here that no one likes at all! I'm not even going to entertain him with giving out who he is. The cats in Seattle will know who I'm talking about. This guy is on speed

hooked him up. So now I just don't go there at all.

Then you have these dealers that watch what you buy and the next time you go to the store they have it on the wall for a stupid amount. It's fucking ridiculous. The truth is if it wasn't for us a lot of these records wouldn't be worth shit and just sitting there like the Barry Manilow joints. Then you got these dealers that [claim] they found some breaks for you, and they don't know the first fucking thing about what a break is and play you some crap—no break. Then you got the dealers like this rocker fuck at this shop here that now collects breaks and takes them all home to his personal collection!

**SM:** Any good or interesting stories about any of your experiences digging?

**MS:** Tons, B. I had a fucked up girlfriend I was seeing who got kicked out of Sound Library only to return a year later and start some shit. She acted up in Groove Merchant too! Once we were in New Jersey, and she asked to use the bathroom and the guy said no, they didn't have one. She asked where he went and he said, "In [my] customers' mouth." She replied with, "Me too, but I get paid for it." She then proceeded to go over to the corner of his store and pissed all over the blues section! This motherfucker deserved it though for real. He ran out of the store, jumped in his car, and chased us for blocks until we lost him!

**SM:** When will the latest Conmen joint be out, and what kinds of things can we expect to hear on it?

**MS:** You know, it's funny you ask that because I haven't seen or talked to Jake in at least two months. I ran into him last night and he was loaded! He wouldn't stop talking about my collection and really going on and gassing me up. So we are gonna hook up soon and put some shit together. He has been doing his thing and he's got lots of production coming out. We have had our differences but we're still fam. A lot of my fam get mad at me because I have stirred from sitting in the lab making tracks everyday to just looking for records everyday!

**SM:** Any other music projects upcoming from Mr. Supreme that we need to brace ourselves for?

**MS:** My LP is actually halfway done. I've been real lazy about it. It's called *Soul, Style & Truth* because that's what I'm about and what I represent. I got Boom Bap on it, who just went out on a national tour, you want to watch for these guys. I got Khalil Krysis who just won the big emcee battle out here. I got Black Anger on it. And so on. ◗

To book Mr. Supreme to DJ or to order Conception merchandise, email conception@earthlink.net or visit conceptionrecords.com.

*For those who don't know,* PHILL STROMAN, *aka the Soulman, has repped the art of crate diggin' in such magazines as* Rap Sheet *and* Big Daddy, *and resurrected his "World of Beats" column online at worldofbeats.com. His latest break CD,* Drugs *is on sale now and bangin' at any self-respecting music shop in the free world, or straight from the source at soulman@worldofbeats.com.*

## Mr. Supreme's Top 10 Things I'm Feelin' at the Moment

1.  Mugo "Organize" 7-inch (United World Records)
2.  My two original mint copies of Jackie Robinson "Pussy Footer" 12-inch
3.  Head in the whip
4.  My original "Lialeh" one sheet, soundtrack, and video
5.  Original '70s *Soul Train* episodes
6.  My custom made 500-diamond, platinum medallion of a 45 rpm adapter
7.  Original Banbarra "Shack Up" 12-inch
8.  Head in the whip
9.  My radio show on groovetech.com
10. WAX POETICS

Honorable mention: The Southern Kitchen in Tacoma, Washington

## Mr. Supreme's Cheap Bin Miracles (Just some of many)

Syl Johnson *Dresses Too Short*, 50 cents
Stark Reality *Hoagy Carmichael Workshop*, 50 cents
James Mason *Rhythm Of Life*, $1.00
Bob Azzam *Great Expectations*, $1.00
Soul Swingers "Ca-Ba-Dab" 7-inch, $2.00
The Turner Bros. LP, $2.00

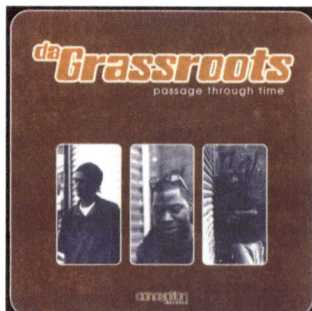

# SOMEWHERE ON THE EAST COAST
## photography by Beth Fladung

# MADLIB: TIGHTLIPPED

Interview by Jon Azpiri
Photos by Eothen Alapatt

## "I got CDs in my crates like crack in my pocket. Yeah right, neither of the above."
### –Lootpack, "Crate Diggin'"

Some people have musical greatness thrust upon them, some are born into it. Otis Jackson Jr.—aka Madlib—has hip-hop embedded into his DNA. His father was an accomplished R&B session musician who played with the likes of David Axelrod and H.B. Barnum. His uncle is Jon Faddis [see fig. 1], legendary trumpeter who played with Dizzy Gillespie, Charles Mingus, and Bob James among others. Growing up, Jackson Jr. was astutely aware of his family's musical legacy. He was obsessed with jazz, hip-hop, and collecting records. These obsessions have worked their way into some of his songs such as Quasimoto's "Jazz Cats, Pt. 1" and "Return of the Loop Digga," a hilariously accurate re-telling of Madlib's run-in with a less-than-knowledgeable record store clerk.

After getting spotted by Peanut Butter Wolf, Madlib was signed to Stones Throw Records. No one could have anticipated the quantity or quality of work that followed. Madlib became the leader of the Lootpack and put out a solo project as his alter-ego Quasimoto, a helium-voiced rapper that Jackson created on a whim and later developed into a full-length album. As if that wasn't enough, he is also the sole member of the new-jazz experiment, Yesterday's New Quintet, which has released a crateload of recordings as of late.

Madlib may have been born into musical greatness, but he also worked his ass off to get where he is. A self-admitted workaholic, Madlib has been known to lock himself in his studio for days at a time. During a rare break between sessions, he took some time to talk about his true loves: hip-hop, crate digging, and jazz.

**When did you start getting into hip-hop?**

In the fourth grade. Breakdancing and stuff. Got into it from then and started buying records.

**When did you start making beats?**

Around '89, I got serious with it. I was always playing around. I started DJing, then I started making beats, then I emceed.

**Of the three—DJing, producing, emceeing—which do you prefer?**

I prefer producing. Believe that. I don't even like to rap too much.

**What's your approach to producing?**

I just try to keep it simple. Basic beat, emcee, and a DJ, you know. I can get wild with it, but right now I'm on some simple-type shit.

**What other producers out there inspire you?**

Of course, Primo. Jay Dee, Soul Brother #1 Pete Rock, DJ Muggs. From the old days I like David Axelrod, Eddie Bo. That's how I want my stuff to be. That old sound. This jazz album I'm working on is like some old shit.

**Have you been in a situation where you used a sample and somebody else uses it six months later?**

All the time. That's why I'm always trying to create new stuff all the time. It's all good. We're all using loops, somebody else is bound to have it. I just try to do it in my way.

**You're heavily into crate digging. You even produced a song with Lootpack about it. How many records do you have?**

Shit, I don't even know. A couple of rooms full.

**Did it start out as a hobby?**

Yeah. I just liked music so I started collecting old jazz records and soul. I wasn't buying too much hip-hop. I used to steal records from universities. I didn't have a lot of money back in the day, I'd get records any way I could. 'Cause I was a true digger, trying to get all that stuff for my collection.

**What kind of stuff did you get from the universities?**

Man, I got all the [David] Axelrod [LPs]. All that stuff that's hard to find. Half them cats weren't even playing that stuff. I'd stay up trying to listen to radio stations and they don't play the stuff.

**My old university had tons of records that no one would listen to.**

Yeah, they don't even listen to the good stuff. I was trying to put it to use for everybody out here.

**So back to Axelrod. What is it about his music that you like so much?**

I like it because it was all dark. It was always funky. It had that soul in it. He'd do other stuff too for other artists. He's got a new album coming out that's dope. I'm trying to be just like that. I want my whole crew to be like that.

**It's amazing how people still hear these old records and still love them. Does that give you hope to know you may have that kind of longevity?**

That's what I hope for more than anything. Hopefully, in thirty years people will like my stuff. That's what I'm striving for.

**When you listen to records are you always looking for beats?**

Nah. I listen to music on the radio, I listen to music from mad crates that I don't even dig from. I just listen.

**Do you ever get that feeling where you hear something and you know you're going to use it in a beat?**

I don't really think about it. I can put a record on and make a beat in five minutes. Just put whatever records I have on and do whatever. It's like freestyle. Try to do it real quick.

**What sort of stuff do you look for?**

I try to get stuff that ain't too popular, like a lot of old independent records, soul records. Rock. Stuff that people ain't really checking for. I go out and buy noise or whatever., rock, classical. I ain't dug in no country yet, but everything else.

**Where do you go looking for beats?**

It's always different for me. The best digging for me is overseas. I got some European stuff that's crazy; funkier than here.

**Where in Europe did you go looking for records?**

I got some stuff in Amsterdam, London. Cats took me to a couple of spots, some swap meets. I bought a bunch of European soundtracks and old stuff. They got a lot stuff that ain't even come out here.

**Do you like reissues?**

I'll take reissues until I get the real one. As long as the music is the same, it's all good.

**What records are on your wish list right now?**

I'm looking for some old records from that cat that did *Fantastic Planet*: some of his old soundtracks. I'm looking for Sun Ra records too. I got a gang of stuff up in my room that I ain't even heard [yet]. I don't try to buy what everybody buys.

**When you go to a record store, do you bring a turntable with you?**

No, that takes the fun out of it. I don't even like to listen to records in the store.

**Do you have a particular place or way you like to listen to records?**

I just put my headphones on and smoke some tree.

**Do you listen to the whole album?**

Nah. Unless it's something that I was looking for; I'll kick back and play it. But if I'm just trying to freestyle beats, I just skip right through it. If you miss some spots and somebody else uses it, years later you'll be like, "Damn, I had that shit."

**One of your best tracks is "Return of the Loop Digga." What inspired that?**

It's about beat shopping. The way homeboy was acting in the store. The same dialogue that's on the record is what

**There's so many young cats out there who don't get jazz. What is it about jazz that speaks to you?**

I don't know. It makes me feel good. The tones, the melodies, and stuff. Different styles.

**You grew up with music all around you.**

Yeah. My dad was a musician. That's all I knew. That's all I did since I was young. Messing around with stuff, turntables and shit.

**What kind of records did your father play on?**

Like, old R&B, '60s, '70s stuff. He did a lot of his own material. Independent stuff. Basically, like what I'm doing now. But he worked with H.B. Barnum who knew cats like the Temptations, the Whispers.

**Your uncle is Jon Faddis. Did you spend a lot of time with him growing up?**

He was always working, but holidays we always spent time at my grandparents. He came down with Dizzy one time. I was battling with Dizzy Gillespie eating gumbo. We was battling to see who could eat the most.

**Has Faddis inspired you?**

That's why I'm doing these jazz albums [Yesterday's New Quintet]. To show him I can do that too. I was trying to get him on this album, but he was so busy, running around

## I used to steal records from universities...Half them cats weren't even playing that stuff. I'd stay up trying to listen to radio stations and they don't play the stuff...I was trying to put it to use for everybody out here.

happened. It happened at a record outlet down in Thousand Oaks. Some people who work in record stores know only one type of music and they're supposed to know all.

**When you go digging, what are some of your favorite labels to look for?**

I like Cobblestone. Prestige. I like Embryo—Herbie Mann was on there. Roy Ayers was on there with his early stuff. I like Blue Note. Warner Brothers. Too many.

**Hearing that list makes me think of your song "Jazz Cats, Pt. 1" where you list some of your favorite jazz artists.**

That song is just one little part. There's like six parts to that. That's the first one. There's some mad names I didn't mention.

**Like who?**

There's too many. Lester Young, Lee Morgan, Anthony Williams, Elvin Jones, Eddie Henderson. I could name all night. I'm letting people know to buy some of that stuff. Some of the names I mention, maybe some cats will peep them.

**What music are you into outside of crate digging?**

I like all types of music, but I'm always listening to jazz.

different countries. He's got a new album coming out and he's touring everywhere.

**Where do you see yourself at that age?**

I see myself doing what I'm doing now. Hopefully, with a little more cash. [*laughs*] I want to keep doing what I'm doing. I'm in the studio every day. I feel like I don't have much time here, so I have to do as much as I can. ●

JON AZPIRI *is a freelance writer from Vancouver, Canada. He divides his time equally between covering sports and music and has written for* SLAM, Inside Stuff, The Source, XXL, Seattle Weekly, *and the* Vancouver Sun.

*fig. 1*

# ON THE BLACKHAND SIDE:

## BLAXPLOITATION AND THE SUBVERSIVE

### BY MARK RANDOLPH

Black-oriented films of the 1970s (commonly known by the NAACP-coined term *blaxploitation*) were part of a very important time in history—cinematically, and as it turns out, philosophically and politically. Created in the political and social turmoil of the post-MLK civil rights era, many of these films often expressed what brothers on the street from Watts to Newark were seeking: redemption. Filled with fast-paced action, the plot usually involved a male hero, or antihero, who found it necessary to renounce the system and resort to violence. Though often maligned for being too violent and fostering stereotypical and simplistic views of Blacks and "ghetto" life (by groups such as the NAACP and CORE, and psychologist and *The Cosby Show* consultant Alvin Poussaint), others saw redeeming qualities in these films. Many saw them as a chance for Blacks to see a semblance of their own lives, struggles, and environments onscreen.

As the pioneering and maverick writer-director of *Sweet Sweetback's Baadasssss Song*, Melvin Van Peebles, put it, "The black audience finally gets a chance to see some of their own fantasies acted out. [It's] about rising out of the mud and kicking some ass." *A badass nigger is about to collect some dues.* Using fast-cut editing in his directing style, soundtrack music, and dialogue (some of which has been sampled on KMD's *Black Bastard* and more recently by Madlib on Quasimoto's *The Unseen*), Van Peebles led the way toward a new style. Hollywood had no choice but to take notice of the power of the Black moviegoing public who grew increasingly tired of the new Negro image being thrust upon them by hackneyed Hollywood vehicles for the Ebony Saint of Tinseltown, Sidney Poitier. His emasculated and feminized roles in several movies such as *Lillies of the Valley* and the notorious *Guess Who's Coming to Dinner* is the yin to the yang of the take-charge violence and sexuality of Black heroes of the new era. This never-before-seen Black hero was sexy and cool, and lived by his own rules outside of the whyte male patriarchal system.

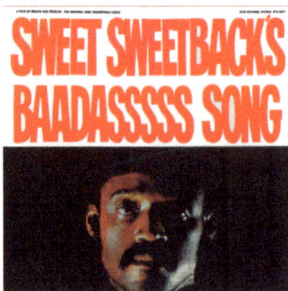

The question is, what of the much-maligned image often portrayed in these films? Are they indeed negative and highly destructive stereotypes or are they a political act-one that actually recontextualizes these stereotypes? The image of the Black hero/antihero that lives and functions outside of the parameters of whyte "civilized" society (which was first portrayed in *Sweet Sweetback's Baadasssss Song* and later in Gordon Parks Jr.'s *Superfly*) became a prototype for the majority of other protagonists in subsequent films. Variations on the aforementioned character were the pimp and the hustler (crimelord, con man).

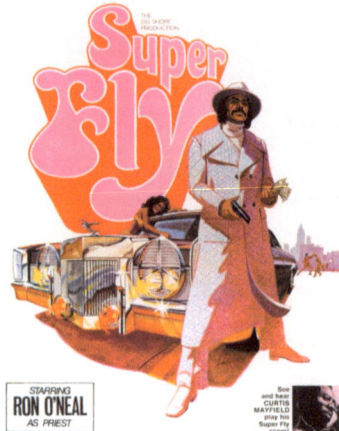

Because blaxploitation films featured pimps and hustlers, these films contained sex and violence, virtually unheard of in earlier urban-themed films—mainly because it was feared by a whyte America, where sex and violence equals power. This attitude was reaffirmed in the early days of hip-hop when FBI probes threatened the West Coast group NWA, and Tipper Gore and the *liberal right* challenged 2 Live Crew and their constitutional rights. Black male power was on display and had to be shut down at all costs.

Power was a key theme in many of these films and was a product of the times in which they were born. The late 1960s and early 1970s saw the Black Power and Black arts movements emerge in America. The Black Panthers were very influential to the growth of the early films in the genre, and vice versa, as members were told to watch *Sweet Sweetback's Baadasssss Song* to understand and visualize what they were fighting for and against. They were fighting for rights as American citizens, and violence was a tool to be used if necessary.

The philosopher, revolutionary, and psychologist Frantz Fanon saw violence as the only way to overthrow a repressive colonial government. Of course Blacks in America were never colonized like the subjects Fanon speaks of in his seminal work, *The Wretched of the Earth*, but were the victims of internal colonization. Fanon had this to say about the necessity of violence in revolution: "At the level of individuals, violence is a cleansing force. It frees the native from his inferiority complex and from his despair and inaction; it makes him fearless and restores his self-respect" (94).

These films can be viewed as visual metaphor for the dawn of a new day and the shape of things to come: a cinematic blueprint for an organized movement of the people towards a united goal. Not your more obvious beret-and-black-jacket revolution, this would be a grassroots movement culled from all walks of life. The hustler, the thug, and the pimp would all take up arms at the dawn of this new era. Whether you were on the corner or in the classroom, the enemy was a common one.

For many at the time, particularly Black youth, these films were something to be proud of. For the first time, identifiable images—good and bad—appeared on screens across the country. Critics (Blacks as well as whites) focused on the detrimental aspects of glorifying thieves, hustlers, and pimps, while failing to see that, by presenting these characters on screen, the filmmakers were truly committing a revolutionary and subversive act. These characters snubbed their collective noses at the whyte patriarchal superstructure.

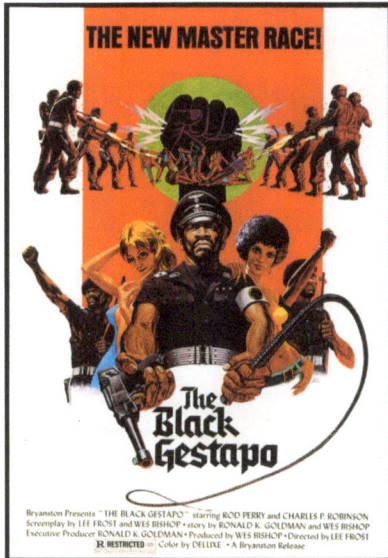

The image of the sexualized Negro had been thrust upon people of African descent for decades in film—such as the bestial savage in *Birth of a Nation* (1915). These notions of Otherness are necessary to create a hierarchy within the whyte system. With the Black man cast in the role of super-sexualized and irrational savage, the benefactors of the whyte male superstructure are free to assert and reaffirm their supposed dominance intellectually. But the pimp and the revolutionary become viable threats when his power is used outside the framework of the dominant system.

This is not to say all blaxploitation films had a Black agenda in mind or had a positive outcome for the Black Power movement. When something makes a substantial profit, the Hollywood machine cranks out similar prod-

ucts: each one more sensational and less substantial than the next. I'm sure Hollywood took notice of the political and cultural ramifications of presenting subversive images onscreen at such a volatile time in our nation's history. Henceforth came films like *Black Gestapo* (1975), which lampooned the Black Liberation movement (even as the movement waned due to years of effective COINTELPRO harassment), and *Mandingo* (1975), which essentially reduced Slavery to a sexy nighttime soap opera.

Ultimately, blaxploitation cinema maintained its relevancy despite hokey plots and half-baked stereotypes presented in many of the lesser films of the genre. Poetry, urban culture, and musical tradition borrowed, as well as incorporated, many themes and images first presented in the most important of these films. From the proto-rap of former Last Poet Lightnin' Rod's 1973 album *Hustler's Convention* (which featured Pretty Purdie and Kool & the Gang), all the way up to Snoop Doggy Dogg's 1993 debut album *Doggystyle* (which had blaxploitation favorite *Dolemite* sampled on the record, as well as Rudy Ray Moore's character guest-starring in the video for "Doggy Dogg World"), the images and styles presented in these films became ingrained in the late twentieth century urban street culture.

In future issues of WAX POETICS, I'll explore the complex relationship between various blaxploitation films and urban philosophy and theory, as well as unearth and review films of the genre that were previously not well known. Through this extensive exploration, I hope to elevate the genre beyond its B-movie status and illuminate the various important cultural and political ideas presented in many of these films. ⬤

MARK ANTHONY RANDOLPH *is an artist and writer from Brooklyn, New York. A graduate from CUNY-Brooklyn, he is currently working on an installation for a gallery exhibition in New York.*

# Outlaw Nation
## or Why Johnny Wants to Be the Next "American Badass"

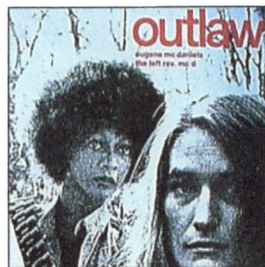

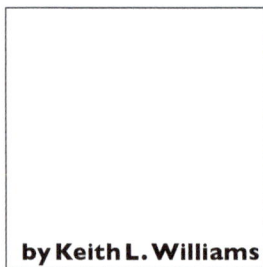

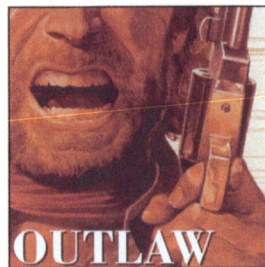

by Keith L. Williams

OUTLAW

"Nowwww, here's a little story I got to tell / about three bad brothas ya know so well /
It started way back in history…" –Beastie Boys, "Paul Revere"

And you know the rest. Or do you? Do you know the history of this great outlaw nation known as the United States of America? At a time when social and political forces point their collective finger at hip-hop culture as the crucible of criminality within the lives of young people, I am always fascinated by the omission of any reference to the fact that we are a nation that was created by outlaws. I've said it—let it be spoken long and aloud. America is a nation by the criminals, of the criminals, and for the criminals.

And it all began on that fateful day of July 4, 1776, the day that United States of America was borne of a criminal act. The men who signed the Declaration of Independence committed the capital offense of sedition and treason against the British Crown. For their participation in such treachery, each man who penned his name on the document—from John Hancock to Benjamin Franklin—would have received a fair trial followed by a first-class hanging. When these gentlemen drafted the deal we have with ourselves called the Constitution, they were very interested in protecting themselves from abuses of authority. Thus from its inception, America has been a country that, to say the least, views law enforcement with extreme skepticism.

The fascination people have with outlaw types is nothing new. The American people have always demonstrated a macabre interest in the lives of outlaws, pirates, gangsters, thugs, robbers, murderers, and downright dirty motherfuckers. At first, the public was rapt by swashbucklers like Edward "Blackbeard" Teach. Noted rebel slaves John Brown and Denmark Vescey were certainly outlaws to

American Southern states hell-bent and whiskey-bound to keep the immoral practice of slavery alive. Next comes the Wild West, where the outlaw is elevated to near-mythic status, with the superhuman figures Jesse James, William "Billy the Kid" Bonney, Wyatt Earp, Geronimo, and Pancho Villa. Images of the pirate outlaw or the Western gunslinger evoke feelings of a frontier America full of adventure, full of possibility.

After the turn of the twentieth century, the outlaw became refined. Organized crime helped many members of this nation maintain an outlaw status through their provision of illegal alcoholic beverages. Notorious bank robbers like Bonnie and Clyde, John Dillinger, and Baby Face Nelson dominated national headlines with their daring heists and getaways. American fascination with the organized crime outlaw captivates the spirit of the culture as much today as during the height of Prohibition, as the awards and accolades of HBO's *The Sopranos* can attest. From Luciano to Gotti, organized crime outlaws keep us riveted with tales of bloodlust and gore. Who hasn't walked by Sparks Steak House in Manhattan without trying to visualize the image of Paul Castellano getting whacked, capped, or given the dirt nap?

Modern popular culture is rife with glorified images of the outlaw. Stories about street life by Iceberg Slim or Donald Goines, or movies such as *Scarface* (both the 1932 Al Capone version and Oliver Stone's 1983 over-the-top classic featuring Al Pacino as Cocaine Superman Tony Montaña) and *The Godfather* all contribute to our muted celebrations for the man who succeeds in spite of the law. People's sense of powerlessness is vicariously overcome through the outlaw's sense of justice as *Goodfellas'* Henry Hill pistol-whips the neighbor kid for getting frisky with his woman. And the audience didn't think "Call the cops" as M.C. Eiht queried, "Yo, homey, you need some help?" before dispensing some frontier justice in *Menace II Society*.

Many hip-hop artists come from a personal situation best described as hard times. Poverty, crime, despair, and economic hardship are not just an abstraction to be studied for their detrimental effects on the person; these are realities of life for many young Black and Hispanic people. Think of the words of Run-D.M.C. in their 1983 debut single: "Unemployment at a record high/people coming, people going, people born to die/don't ask me because I don't know why/but it's like that"; or Melle Mel's lyrics in "The Message."

Sadly enough, that reality has not changed for most Black or Hispanic people. In that reality, the outlaw is a sentient being; he is as real as the circumstances that create him. As a fixture on every corner in the neighborhood, he represents, for many residents, the only method of success attainable by someone whose neighborhood lacks adequate schools, businesses, or other social, economic, and political institutions that provide opportunities for advancement. The outlaw becomes the ultimate hero and the ultimate rebel. He is seen as an individual who uses his wits and nerve to make it in spite of the odds against him and does so without apology because for him to accept the lot the world has given him makes him a failure. America is premised upon one's ability to rise above any station in life, and those who do not desire to rise above that station are seen as possessing a loser's attitude. Accordingly, those persons are despised as the lowest form of humanity—someone who'll accept being treated like a jerk.

Hip-hop, as a music and culture, is built on a rebellion that is directly caused by the lack of inclusion of inner-city youth by society. Hip-hop artists, because of many parallel situations in which they find themselves, have much in common with the outlaw (or may *be* the outlaw) and may therefore identify more with the outlaw than with a citizen in society's mainstream. Early hip-hop outlaws like DJ Kool Herc stole electricity to provide music for illegal street parties. Ghetto celebrities like Coke La Rock and Eddie Cheeba emceed parties with stage names that professed their love for illegal drugs. Real-life outlaw heroin dealers like Nicky Barnes and Pappy Mason gave away turkeys in Harlem on Thanksgiving (inspiring the scene in *New Jack City*).

Like the heroes of so many Black action films of the last thirty-odd years (lumped together under the demeaning banner of blaxploitation), the outlaw always goes for what he knows, and, at times, comes out on top. Whether it's Sweetback, "Superfly" Priest, Goldie the Mack, Dolemite, or Rhyggin (the real Jamaican two-gun outlaw who served as the basis for Jimmy Cliff's *The Harder They Fall*), the outlaw who prevails or dies trying is embraced by many hip-hop artists. Either the artist is (or was) an outlaw in the legal sense, or a musical outlaw who refused to accept the status quo and stuck it to the "Man" of the music industry á la Public Enemy.

Being a person who possesses a hard outlaw mentality is a common theme repeated by many artists. Schoolly D., the Geto Boys, NWA, Kool G. Rap, and Ice-T based their careers on an assumed outlaw role. The indiscriminately violent caricature created by Cypress Hill's "How I Could Just Kill a Man" or "Hand on the Pump" evokes images of the Wild West outlaw John Wesley Harding, who reputedly shot a man for snoring too loud. In 1994's "Represent," Nas proclaims, "They call me Nas, I'm not your legal type of fella/Moët drinkin', marijuana smokin' street dwella"; similar to Ghostface Killah's declaration: "I used to be in Job Corps/now I'm an outlaw/Ray Cartegena/carry a fo'-fo'," in "Can It Be All So Simple" (remix). The outlaw is not just embraced lyrically but also spiritually by many who adopt the moniker of their favorite bad man, both real and fictional (Scarface, Capone-N-Noreaga, Nas Escobar, Joe Cartegena, Lex Diamonds, Biggie Smalls, Ice-T, or anybody with "Mack" as a part of their name). It matters not that all these "bad men" were captured or killed—the embodiment of the outlaw spirit means one must have a willingness to give his life before bending to unjust forces. For in America, 'tis more noble to fight the Man and die than to never put up a fight at all. As stated so eloquently by M.O.P.'s Billy Danze in "Stick to Ya Gunz," "If it happen, the squad's cappin'/I'm in the mix/and I'd rather be judged by twelve than laid by six."

So to say today's hip-hop artists somehow singularly corrupt the "youth of America" with their fantastic stories of outlaw behavior is only a cop-out for people who need an easy, disenfranchised target for their prepackaged political venom. The fact is that the American public is fascinated by outlaws and many have dreamt of being one at some point. At the very least, we exercise no restraint in observing the outlaw's car crash of a life like some lurid fantasy, enjoying the tale even as it shivers us. Whether it was the lure of seemingly easy money or the lure of the "life"—as the criminal lifestyle is referred to in outlaw circles—there is something that seems both attractive and liberating about residing outside the boundaries of legality. It speaks to the realization of the freedoms we always state that we have in America. It stands for the complete rejection of unjustified authority that is the symbol of our "One Nation." The fact that artists such as Raekwon the Chef, Kool G. Rap, Ice-T., Ghostface Killah, J.T. Money, Scarface, and Too Short paint such vivid images of criminal lifestyle is not the cause of the outlaw culture—their words are merely its reflection. ◉

KEITH L. WILLIAMS, ESQ. *lives in Florida and practices law. He has previously done time as a hip-hop radio jock, frontman for the now hibernating crew SPLADOW, and has authored articles for* Bomb *and* Moon *magazines. He spends his free time creating interludes and answering machine messages from old radio serials, Westerns, and Mafioso movies, and is currently working on the first hip-hop record to sample exclusively from radio, film, and television (including all musical and spoken parts).*

# AFRONAUTS
### for Adam Banks

## BY THOMAS SAYERS ELLIS

Night's nightmarish record-vinyl darkness,
      wild stylus outrageous and rooted in reflector.
A pillbox of plantations, even bigger cotton,
      and wades of shock
folk like us wave off. Unsleeved plastic,
      both flat black sides
      a single and a signal

double conscious as stereo,
      afro-modernity's unfinished triangular
soul auction-troped ear—less landlessness,
      the not yet black Black Atlantic's
over crisscrossed dynamic traffic.
      Phat black similes, phat black smiles,
      phat black miles.

Any number of syncretic speakers spanking
      and spankers speaking
—unchartable rhythm rhythm rhythm
      going 'round the needle's shark-like patience.
The universe, a panasonic dancefloor,
      plaidabout stars.
      Well what, if not memory, is orbit?

Section Eights, double platinum ones,
      black minds already know,
all economically and diasporically looped.
      Shoes, unlike the sun, always OFF.
Pelvic dress and walk,
      sweet badass bounce.
      *Ohh!* Space memory of running,

for one's life,
      overboard into race.

THOMAS SAYERS ELLIS *is the author of* The Good Junk *(in* Take Three, *Graywolf Press 1996) and* The Genuine Negro Hero *(Kent State University Press, 2001). He has a poem in* The Best American Poetry 2001 *and poems forthcoming in* Tin House.

*Brooklyn multimedia artist* RONALD P. EDWARDS, *aka* STOZO THE CLOWN, *is a long-time collaborator with Parliament-Funkadelic. Stozo's artwork has graced the covers of recording artists such as Fuzzy Haskins, ZAPP, and Fred Wesley. Also a tireless musician, he is currently working on his upcoming album,* Welcome to Stozo's Land, *featuring the late Eddie Hazel, Shuggie Otis, and others. "Afronauts" is part of a collaborative series between T. S. Ellis and Stozo.*

# Re:Discovery

## Bwana *Bwana* (Caytronics, 1972: CYS 1312)

by J. P. Jones

The bulk of our personal sound libraries contain only one or two breaks; most of our records aren't start-to-finish gemjams. These pieces constitute the main volume of our crates and greatly reflect who we are when we're spinning for the crowd or building beats in the studio. They're the groovegrapes that make up your flavor—ears taste you and heads nod (*mmm*) or nod (*zzz*). You pull out the disc for its Something Sweet then it's back in box. Mixer style is also a major invocation of your rep, but it all starts with the numerous "it's-got-*this*" jewels of your dig efforts.

Hoarding unwieldly amounts of albums means some Extra Special Platters easily get lost in the DJ shuffle. (Damn, some get *lost*.) In each issue, "Re:Discovery" will expose some full-on treats you might find in your collection, records that are more than simple one-track ponies, bombs from drop to run-out and worth your forty+ minutes of leisure eartime. Some are relentlessly funky; effortlessly soulful; endlessly challenging; or just damn wicked. These discs aren't just for sampling—you can savor all their wares with delight from beginning to end.

There's something naughty about the kid caricature on the cover of *Bwana*—did somebody say "Sambo"? Nah—the young brother's got a peace sign medallion around his neck and sandals on his feet. It's Hippie Child! Closer aural inspection divulges this visual image is a reflection of the childlike energy and sense of adventure contained in the wax—his young Latin American muchachos produce joyous and soulful Latin love. This eponymously titled album mixes up hot percussion-based jams with suggestive Afro-Indio spices and a generous suggestion of American soulfunk appropo of the vintage. Make no mistake: This is a jam record. But it's that rare combination of tasteful yet engaging. Relatively few Latin albums hold up your interest over the course of forty minutes like *Bwana* does, and the cause is greatly helped by the fact these musicians feel the funk with a palpable feel of searching adventure. Darting organ runs; infectious percussion workouts; get-you-moving bass; gentle blaxploitation wah-wah backup rhythm guitar whiffs; searing tight psych-esque leads—*Bwana* makes ya *wanna*.

From the first declaration, "Teme de Bwana" (of course!), with its forceful propulsive percussion/organ opening salvo, there's no question drummer Donaldo Mantilla and percussionists Salvador Fernandez and Roman Corpas have a most serious funky Barretto jones to work out together. They all meld spaces effortlessly, the earmark of the finer Latin superclassic albums. As evidenced on this song and throughout *Bwana*, guitarist/leader Roberto Martinez infuses nimble leads and runs with a late-'60s Santana influence, also managing to incorporate some African highlife touches. He has great instinctual feel for what his bandmates are laying down, and they respond in kind. And I do mean *kind*.

The last cut on side one, "Chapumbambe," is the track best known to beatheads. It starts off with the requisite Nice Break; then the band stretches out, giving good time to Martinez, organist/occasional second guitarist Ricardo Palma, and of course the three-head *batteria*, contributing deep enough to be interesting but never busy-bang-banging to distraction. The band vocally invokes the title twice, first signaling the start of a stunning fuzzed-out Martinez solo, then again to give Mantilla, Fernandez, and Corpas some skintime. (The panning here gently swirls clockwise for a very cool headphone moment.) Eventually the song winds up with a sparse spacey freakout, waiting for some electrohead to bite and reconfigure. It's nyce when a record adds a little way-out on their way out.

"Motemba," first track side two, leads off with a low-tuned bongo/tambale figure, joined up with an Indio-inspired organ line courtesy of Ricardo Palma. Minutes before they fade and exit, the group switches up the bounce with a slower swagger, highlighted by some sweet afrofunk guitar chording. This segues perfectly with the next tune, "Todo es Real," as it begins with a bit of high-lifelike chunk-a chunk-a; this gives way to a spicy Turkish-flavored Farfisa line and some totally kickass sneaky-snakey ride cymbal work. Before long, the group takes "Todo es Real" to Another Level with a "Witchy Woman"/"Stormy"-styled backbeat and some very effective forceful singing in English (only one of two songs on the album to feature full vocals). Martinez lays down two short 'n' sweethot solos, the second time signaling a change back to the original beat before they out. A cornucopia of magic—all in a shade of just over five minutes!

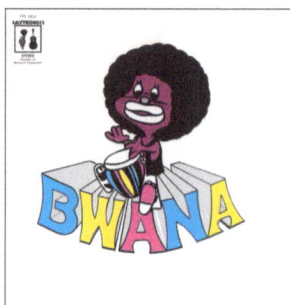

The record concludes with "Lolita," which glides with an up-smooth R&B feel and some playfully sung lyrics in their native language. Guitar snatches, organ wash swashes, and hopping bassbops are once again driven by the Bwana trademark of simple-but-direct percussion work, ultimately winding down the album with quiet kinetic energy.

The immediacy of the recording atmosphere throughout *Bwana* is such that you can sometimes hear the clicking of the organ keys; palms slapping the sides of the tumbas; fingers sliding on guitar necks, thus capturing a vital of-the-moment essence. Repeated listenings reveal these talented musicians effortlessly melding their individual strengths into a focused, cohesive sound. Their combined avoidance of overindulgence in their experimentation is a major plus for a record of its genre. It's our loss Bwana only managed to release this one record. Fortunately for our earspace, this leaves room for many more hardhitters. ◗

J. P. JONES *was a founding member of Lynnfield Pioneers, best known for their groundbreaking album* Free Popcorn *(Matador Records).*

# The Academic Archive: Volume I

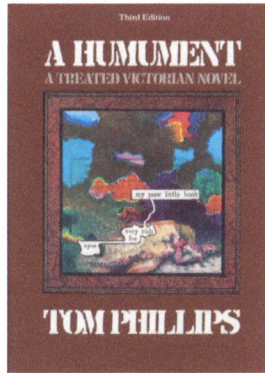

Text by Joe Allen

W hen discussing record hunting in an article about beatdigging in *Life Sucks Die*, Mr. Supreme said, "I'm like a magnet to breaks!…I can just pick up any record and it will have a beat." Because of the many ways to employ samples, I have heard other producers express similar sentiments. I identify with this uncanny serendipity although not necessarily with records. Besides collecting records, I have been accumulating other source material that resembles either the cut and mix aesthetic of hip-hop or the impulse to collect; my archive includes everything from the collages of Romare Bearden and the cultural theory of Walter Benjamim to novels such as Ishmael Reed's *Mumbo Jumbo* and Nathaniel Mackey's *Djbot Baghostus's Run*. Everywhere I turn, more hip-hop manifestations rise to the surface. In fact, the very day I came across the Mr. Supreme quote, I was reading the first novel, *City of Glass*, of Paul Auster's postmodern detective series, *The New York Trilogy*. The novel has very little to do with the practice of sampling—the closest relationship might be the fragmentary nature of identity or the presentation of different and shrouded versions of the same events. Nonetheless, the novel contains a remarkable passage when the detective Quinn first confronts Stillman, the man he has been watching and following aimlessly around New York. Stillman has been writing a book and he explains his compositional strategy:

> My work is very simple. I have come to New York because it is the most forlorn of places, the most abject. The brokenness is everywhere, the disarray is universal. You only have to open your eyes to see it. The broken people, the broken things, the broken thoughts. The whole city is a junk heap. It suits my purposes admirably. I find the streets an endless source of material, an inexhaustible storehouse of shattered things. Each day I go out with my bag and collect objects that seem worthy of investigation. My samples now number in the hundreds—from the chipped to the smashed, from the dented to the squashed, from the pulverized to the putrid. (94) [1]

I thought I was reading about digging for beats and samples; not about the way writers absorb and sample source material. As the Auster quote suggests, though, the process has a striking relationship.

In each issue of WAX POETICS, this column will discuss the relationship between the hip-hop practice of record collecting and sampling to other art, literature, and theory. Such multi-disciplinary comparisons will place the hip-hop aesthetic in a larger cultural, historical, and artistic context. Just as the Aretha Franklin sample on Mos Def's "Ms. Fat Booty" has caused many of us to check Aretha's beautiful track "One Step Ahead," hopefully the Academic Archive will inspire a few readers to track down a different kind of source material.

First up is a painter, writer, and composer from London, Tom Phillips, and his lifelong project *A Humument: A Treated Victorian Novel* (1980, first edition; 1987, first revised edition; 1997, second revised edition), which draws inspiration from William Burroughs's much noted cut-up technique. But rather than cut up his own work, Phillips initially sought to *rework* and *retextualize* the first coherent book he could find for threepence[2]: he found *A Human Document* (by W. H. Mallock, published in 1892) on "a routine Saturday morning shopping expedition."[3] Phillips describes his technique at the end of his second revised edition: "I merely scored out unwanted words with pen and ink," thereby creating poetic fragments that read down the page. Then, "It was not long though before the possibility became apparent of making a better unity of word and image, intertwined as in a medieval miniature." Thus, Phillips employed painting, rendering many of the 368 pages into stunningly beautiful and unique watercolor or gouache paintings that surround, highlight, and incorporate the leftover text [*see fig. 1*]. His resulting text contains "poems, music scores, parodies, notes on aesthetics, autobiography, concrete texts, romance, mild erotica, as well as the undertext of Mallock's original story." According to Phillips, *A Humument* "is a reasonable example of *bricolage*, and…perhaps a massive *deconstruction* job taking the form of a curious unwitting collaboration between two ill-suited people seventy-five years apart." Phillips's compositional technique unquestionably shares much with the practice of hip-hop sampling: signifying on an original work of art, chopping, and then *recontextualizing* pieces of the original, adding new layers, and ultimately assembling a new work of art.

Phillips has continued to revise his work by first publishing ten smaller volumes and now three editions (each revised) of the entire work. When he began varying his original text, he had to find a second copy of Matlock's novel. The copy he found "had belonged to one Lottie Yates who had herself 'treated' it to some extent, heavily underlining passages that seemed to relate to her own romantic plight. … Thus, in 1902, someone had already started to work the mine." How many times do we go back to the archetypal beats and breaks only to mine them again and uncover untouched possibilities (see Q-Bert's mix tape *Pre School Break Mix*)?

With two more volumes, Phillips will have completely overhauled his first edition. Because each page has such a "rich set of alternatives," he has proved to himself the "inexhaustibility of even a single page" by producing over twenty variations of page 85 [*see fig. 2*]. In the third edition of *A Humument*, Phillips even samples his previous editions, as he says, "In some recent pages I have incorporated elements of their printed predecessors." For instance, the painting on page 105 includes a picture on the wall which is "made from fragments" of the original edition of the page [*see fig. 3*]. Hip-hop artists aren't the only composers who sample their own work (see Diamond D: "I took a blues break and I broke it").

With a digital sampler, a song, sample, or break can be altered and re-altered in a similar fashion. Phillips's com-

ments are reminiscent of the endless possibilities of use of the inexhaustible archive of recorded and found sounds. Although hip-hop producers have sampled other mediums, the medium of choice remains the vinyl LP. Rob Corrigan of the Sound Library record store in NYC believes that most beats and funky loops have been uncovered—a testament to the research capabilities of the legions of beat-diggers. Yet, he comments, "We won't run out of samples. We've reached that point where every record, every kind of music is sampable." Noted producer Showbiz agrees: "There's a lot of different sounds out there, a lot of different records that haven't been touched" (qtd. in Soulman's "World of Beats Vol. 4a"). For instance, Soulman's latest mix *Neva Stop Diggin'* contains a track of breaks and loops culled from Spanish records. DJ Premier adds that the "underground will live forever," knowing full well that he and others (see the People Under the Stairs' *Question in the Form of an Answer*) will proceed to dig for samples, cutting and chopping small bits and pieces of sounds until a new sound takes shape. ◉

JOE ALLEN *is an Assistant Professor of English at Dutchess Community College in Poughkeepsie, NY. Much of his research has focused on cultural studies including contemporary fiction and music (especially hip-hop). He recently published a chapbook titled* He's the DJ, I'm the Turntablist: The Progressive Art of Hip Hop DJs *on Mississinewa Press. Also, "The Operatic Incongruity of Nathaniel Mackey's* Djbot Baghostus's Run" *will appear in the forthcoming collection of essays* Black Orpheus *on Garland Press.*

Notes:

1. Paul Auster, *City of Glass* (Penguin Books, 1985).
2. The sum of three British pennies [*Webster's*].
3. This and subsequent Tom Phillips's quotes from *A Humument: A Treated Victorian Novel* [Third Edition] (Thames & Hudson, 1997).

Artwork reprinted with permission from the author.

*fig. 1*

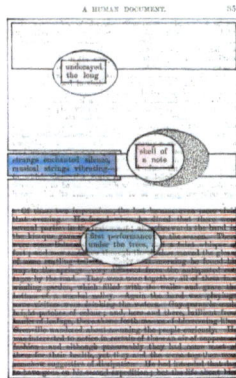

*fig. 2*

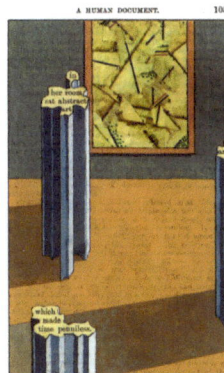

*fig. 3*

# Home Improvement

written and illustrated by Alberto Forero

It starts out small enough: a record here, two records there. First you make a pile near your turntables. Then, the pile gets pretty big and you look for a crate. It seems like the milk company finally got hip to the popularity of milk crates for holding things other than milk, and now all you can find are 10" crates behind your grocery store. I once considered hiring a carpenter to build some wooden shelves or boxes. I mean, how complicated or expensive could that be? Cut the wood, nail it together; you're done, right? Wrong. I called half a dozen places and ended up with quotes from $250 to $800—for six, no frills, 13" plywood cubes. I thought, there has to be a better way. And there is: You do it yourself. I haven't done a lot of carpentry, but I was able to make some nice record cube shelves for about $10 apiece, and here's how.

## Checklist of supplies
### (enough for six record cubes)

- Hammer

- One 8 oz. tube of "PL Premium Wood Glue" or similar ($5)

- One box of "Grip-Rite Fas'ners" 4d or similar 1-½" nails. ($1.50)

- Three 4' x 4', ½" thick plywood sheets ($15 each)

- One 2' x 4', ½" thick plywood sheet ($8)

- An old sheet

## The design

I decided on cubes because they are modular, move around easily, and can form together for different shaped shelving units. Also, with cubes I could have a platform for my tables and mixer as well. And one cube will comfortably fit eighty-five LPs.

I drew out a plan. This was pretty easy, since they're just cubes. I figured I'd need a little extra space at the top to easily get records in and out, so I designed a space 14" high and 13" wide and 13" deep. The side pieces fit between the top and bottom of the cube in a "post and lintel" form [fig. 1], able to support a lot of weight. I designed a cube that had a top, bottom, and back made from 14" x 14" pieces, and the two sides made from 14" x 13" pieces [fig. 2].

**Figure 1**

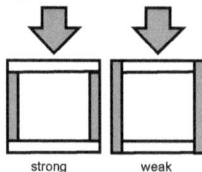

strong        weak

**Figure 2**

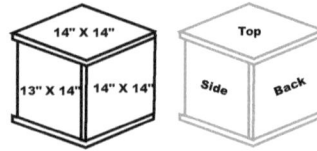

## A trip to the hardware store

I went to Home Depot and saw that wood is nice, but it's expensive and heavy. That's when I checked out the plywood: cheap, sturdy, relatively light, and not bad looking, especially when you're basically seeing only the edges of it. I used ½" thick plywood—you can buy a 4' x 4' sheet for $15, or a 2' x 4' sheet for $8. If you get three of the 4' x 4' sheets and one of the 2' x 4' sheets, you will have enough plywood to make six record boxes, plus have a few extra pieces in case you mess up. That works out to twenty 14" x 14" pieces and thirteen of the 14" x 13" pieces once cut. Home Depot charges fifty cents per cut, so for six boxes, you're looking at about $12 in cutting charges. Bring a diagram showing exactly how you want the wood cut [fig. 3].

**Figure 3**

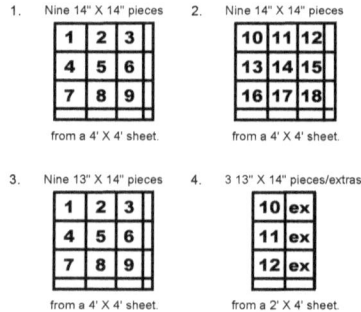

1. Nine 14" X 14" pieces — from a 4' X 4' sheet.
2. Nine 14" X 14" pieces — from a 4' X 4' sheet.
3. Nine 13" X 14" pieces — from a 4' X 4' sheet.
4. 3 13" X 14" pieces/extras — from a 2' X 4' sheet.

## Putting the cube together, step by step

When you're constructing the cubes, it's good to lay an old sheet or towel on the ground so that you don't get the glue all over the place. But watch that the boxes don't dry connected to the sheet. I also found it helpful to mark the connecting ends of the pieces with an x. The pieces look pretty similar, so it's good to put the box together methodically. Once you make one, however, it's pretty obvious. When attaching each piece, I picked the better-looking side, one with less splinters or dirt, and placed it facing outside. Don't worry if you hammer a nail in and see it start to come out the side of the wood—just pull it out and start over a ¼" from where you were hammering—you probably won't see the original hole because you're not looking at the inside or the side of the cube. And if you leave that sharp nail sticking out on the inside, you run the risk of slicing up that mint copy of Afro-Harping you just found for fifty cents at a garage sale.

Make sure that the edges of your box are as level as possible and line up at nice tight corners. The guy who was cutting my wood cut a few of pieces a ½" off or so, but I found that with a little careful positioning, almost all of my boxes were solid (no gaps at edges), and, again, if your box is slightly off, no one's ever going to notice.

1. Take the back piece (14" x 14") and hold it vertically **[fig. 4]**.

**Figure 4**

2. Add a thin line of glue on the top edge of the back piece.

3. Place the top piece (14" x 14") on top of the back piece and line it up with the back edge. To keep the top piece level, temporarily prop another 14" x 14" piece under the front edge **[fig. 5]**.

**Figure 5**

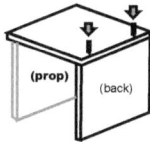

4. Holding the top piece perpendicular to the back piece, hammer one nail through the top into the center of the back piece, about 2" from each side.

5. Place a side piece (14" x 13") against the top and back. There should be a ½" lip of the top reaching over the side; that's fine—it will be a little dust cover on the front of your box. Add a thin line of glue on the top and the side of this piece, press it into the top and back, and then hammer in nails 2" from each edge on top, watching to make sure that things stay lined up **[fig. 6]**. Then turn the box with the back side up, and hammer two more nails to connect the back and side piece.

**Figure 6**

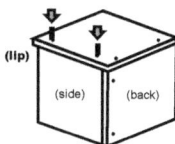

6. Do the same thing for the other side.

7. Flip your box on its top, and add glue around the three edges **[fig. 7]**.

8. Take the bottom piece (14" x 14") and place it opposite the top to complete the box **[fig. 7]**.

**Figure 7**

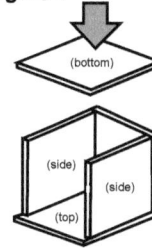

9. Hammer two nails in each of the three sides **[fig. 8]**.

**Figure 8**

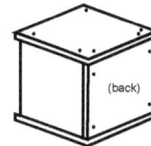

10. Now that you have the box put together, apply a thin line of glue on every inside edge of the box, just to make it extra sturdy.

11. Set the box aside. Once the glue is relatively dry (thirty minutes), put a pile of records or books on top of the box, just to make sure that the pieces dry firmly together.

12. The finished box **[fig. 9]**.

**Figure 9**

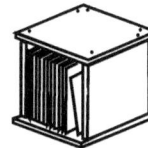

**Notes:**
Don't put the records in before the glue has completely dried or they'll never leave the box; let the glue dry over night. I found that I put a bit too much glue on the first time, which then left hard bumps on the insides of the box, making it harder to slide records in easily. I recommend using a minimum of glue (the nails will suffice). You could always sand off excess glue later—but this is supposed to be a simple project. It took me about an hour to put together the first box, but the others went faster. If the hammering gets too noisy, you can put an old towel or sheet in the box, drummer style, to muffle the sound a bit. (Unfortunately, this didn't stop me from getting a noise complaint.) And you can stain or paint the cubes if you are more ambitious.

www.ingramcontent.com/pod-product-compliance
Lightning Source LLC
Chambersburg PA
CBHW040750100426
42735CB00035B/142